Sexuality, Relationships and
Spiritual Growth

I0022356

By the same author
The Family Repairs and Maintenance Manual

Sexuality, Relationships and Spiritual Growth

by

Agnes Ghaznavi

GR

GEORGE RONALD
OXFORD

George Ronald, Publisher

© Agnes Ghaznavi 1995
All Rights Reserved

A Cataloguing in Publication entry
is available from the British Library

ISBN 0–85398–382–8

Cover painting
'Awaiting the Dawn'
by Richard Morgan

Contents

Foreword   ix

1. The daily practice of a psychiatrist   I
   Sexual identity: A story of generations   8
   A story of apples   9

2. Traditional attitudes looming over the present   12
   "The man in my life"   17

3. Qualities and attitudes necessary in a relationship
   of equality   20

   Reciprocity   21
   Respect   25
   Friendship   25
   Loyalty   29
   Chastity   30
   Fidelity   38
   Closeness and freedom   41
   Tenderness   44
   Affection   48

4. Some difficult relationships   51
   Jealousy   52
   Envy   53

v

Having to be right	54
The sensitive and the insensitive	55
The spendthrift and the tightfisted	56
The orderly and the "artistic"	57
The hyper-sexual and the prudish	58
The oppositional character	59
The partner as garbage bin	59
Sado-masochistic relationships	60
Some other pathological relationships	63
5. Immature and degrading relationships	66
Three wheels . . .	66
Incestuous relationships and sexual abuse	70
Perversion and the fear of it	83
6. Pain and development	91
My parents and I	91
On becoming a person	93
Emerging sexuality	99
Vulnerability and anger	102
7. Sexual development	106
Sexual development in children	106
Masturbation	108
Adolescents and sexuality	111
8. Choosing a partner for life	118
On romanticism	121
On commitment	124
9. New aspects of sexuality	133
Relationship	133
Passion and sensuality in love	135
Not suppression, but regulation and control	141
Communication as a model for body and mind	146

Contents

10. New methods of spiritual health   152

    Love as action   152
    They must not keep it in their hearts   154
    Irrigate continually the tree of your union   155
    Facing difficulties   156

Epilogue   160

Bibliography   165

References   167

Foreword

JUST a few decades ago, a silent revolution began — the sexual revolution. And it is not over yet!

More than a century ago, a much more potent revolution took place: a prisoner, the Divine Manifestation, Bahá'u'lláh, proclaimed mankind to be one, and man and woman equal in rights. From then on women have begun to develop their capacities, and opportunities have begun to open up in all kinds of fields of endeavour in the wider society. Thus, the age-old structures of family and societal relationships have begun to crack.

The vision of the Bahá'í Faith is one of evolution and progressive human development, of capacities blossoming in both men and women, of new opportunities offered by an evolving society. It is the vision of a society enriched by those feminine qualities confined up to now within the bounds of the home. This vision speaks of new qualities being woven into intimate bonds between man and woman, while upholding standards of chastity. Chastity will permit people to associate more freely and with great creativity in relationships — whether at work, in leisure, or in creative fields such as the religious, artistic or scientific.

Is there any ready solution, according to psychology, for all the difficulties people are encountering today in their relationships and their sexual aspirations? Up to now I have never come across one that has proven to work durably. Wherever problems have built up the answer has been to combine consultation and the desire to grow both as persons and in the relationship, then to seek adjustment, sexually, in this new context. This is the vision of the Bahá'í Faith.

For those who are determined to follow a new vision in relationships, and thus also in their sexual needs, there is the recompense of personal growth and enrichment of the relationship. The price is hard work — often an intense suffering — combined with a growing feeling of mastery and an opening into new fields of experience, both emotional and spiritual.

There are no quick-fix solutions. I firmly believe the Bahá'í Faith offers the most beautiful "recipe" we can find in our modern age for this complex of relationship growth and sexual needs. Moreover, this recipe doesn't seem in the least to be limited to those who profess to be Bahá'ís, but seems to be universally applicable. Where people are not following this new model, their sexual life comes to a halt, or their relationship loses its richness, or their inner self undergoes suffering and hardship, or emptiness. Human beings are so fragile, hesitant and apathetic in their aspiration to grow and evolve, but everybody seems to be labouring in this spiral, tending one day to inner growth, another to the relationship with the life-companion or attempting to respond to sexual needs — besides the many and complex other developments in our human lives.

In the last resort, all of us seem to have to evolve in the same direction — to grow spiritually and to translate this into attitudes and actions permeating our daily lives.

With this in mind, I'd like to define a few terms as they are used in this book:

The *marital relationship* (relationship for short) is the desire of two persons to interrelate durably and more and more deeply:

. . . marriage must be a union of the body and of the spirit as well
. . . for if the marriage is based both on the spirit and the body, that
union is a true one, hence it will endure. ('Abdu'l-Bahá)[1]

Sexuality is a term denoting a wider sphere than only bodily
functions. Sexuality is complex in its expression and encompasses all levels of the human being — physical, psychological,
social and spiritual. Sexuality and the relationship intertwine,
so to say:

. . . a true relationship between two parties who are fond of one
another . . . both physical and spiritual relationship. ('Abdu'l-
Bahá)[2]

Sex is a human activity.

I

The daily practice of a psychiatrist

MOST people, if they come to think about it, will have learned all kinds of sketchy bits of information about sexuality. Beginning in very early childhood, this informal sex education starts in the family and continues throughout school years and adolescence. Nowadays many schools have formal sex education programmes and there are so many articles in the popular press and books on sexual functioning that it has become difficult to avoid being deluged by information. Yet people remain strangely loyal to their childhood relics: although well-informed, their own sexuality often seems to cling to their early sources of learning, however partial or untrue.

I remember in my own childhood being vaguely aware of an air of tense embarrassment on the part of my parents whenever they had been intimate. This made me wary – I learned tactfully to avoid embarrassing them further – or indeed other people. I learned to pretend not to have understood.

However, my curiosity had been aroused! So I turned to books – all kinds of books – in an effort to gather more information on this mysterious subject which seemed to be for grown-ups only, not for children. I wondered and thought a lot, in an endeavour to fathom the mystery. Later on, the dictionary came to my rescue. My father had bought the very old, very thorough *Grosse Brockhaus* for the family, and this was a welcome source of interesting views and fascinating anatomical detail. Pathology was particularly accurately described.

Handed straight down from my puritanical, pioneering American forefathers came the taboo: "these things" are for men only; a virtuous woman acts as if she has nothing to do with it all. An avid reader of romantic novels, I was struck by the advice of the Victorians to "lie back and think of the legs of the grand piano". Little did I know what this all meant — it was all such a mystery, and so obviously important!

When I began to show the first signs of pre-puberty my mother prepared me for the onset of menstruation. This was a rather terse introduction to the art of having babies. I learned to call my period the "curse" — the normal vocabulary of the time. Girls, I learned, neither swim nor participate in sports when they have "the curse". I felt embarrassed, pin-pointed.

Later on, I was invited by my mother to have a little talk about love. I sat down next to her and the sewing-machine. Mother had obviously taken all her courage in hand and was determined to do her duty by me. Hands in her lap, she began: "When you love a man . . . when you love a man . . . well (here she faltered and then visibly gave up) when you love a man all is well!" Then and there I learned that never, never must I make my mother so unhappy again by showing any interest in knowing more about this mysterious subject! I also learned that what she said was not necessarily the whole truth, but this I kept to myself.

When the time to date had come, I found to my astonishment and dislike that girls, whatever their character and disposition, were told to be careful and distrustful of men, because all of them only wanted one thing. Boys, on the other hand, were encouraged to prove their virility by going out with as many girls as possible and having precocious sexual intercourse: it was not good to get involved in a relationship. This, I learned later, was traditional education: different standards for boys and girls. To my bewilderment, the double standard was being invoked by parents of both boys and girls, thus encouraging boys to be permissive and irresponsible in the name of "freedom", girls to be fearful and defensive. Girls who went along with the boys' wishes were called good sports (by men) but were not thought worth much.

What is the result of all this? More and more people nowadays are bringing their sexual malfunction to the attention of their general practitioner. Women, when consulting a gynaecologist, will pour out volumes of suppressed suffering at the slightest question. Often referred to me by the gynaecologist, women then introduce themselves in the following vein:

"Doctor, I've never felt anything during sexual intercourse. Sometimes, several years ago, I dreamt and woke up having an orgasm. It felt good. But I've never had such a sensation with my husband (or boy-friend). When I read about orgasm I feel left out. Not so long ago, I told my husband about this sorry fact in our married life. He was horrified. I had always faked blissfulness during sexual intercourse. He felt guilty and mortified that he had not been able to give me an orgasm. Since then, things have got steadily worse between us, as my husband is becoming morose at his inability to give me an orgasm. He insisted I come and see you."

Of course, it is not a man's responsibility to "give" a woman an orgasm – that's her own affair. But a man certainly can help a great deal and contribute to it.

Apart from personal and specific advice I often introduce some basic facts about sexuality and then touch on the following aspects:

- Usually, both partners suffer from an immaturity or malfunction of their sexual faculties. The more apparent symptom of the one may hide the other's symptom, as in a man's premature ejaculation and a woman's orgasmic dysfunction.

- Often, people have not had any or only flimsy sexual education. This seems to be the case not only for my small town near the mountains of western Switzerland, but also for women living in cosmopolitan areas. Being well-read or sophisticated changes the level of knowledge but not the sensations! Frank and open discussion on these matters can open barriers of ignorance and resulting fears and thus clear the way for natural sexual flow.

- Also, people's symptoms are anchored in their own personal history and their family's as well, reaching back several generations. Conflicts have built up and grievances have not been ventilated. Longstanding frustration has blocked the relationship and its expression.

- There may also be hidden conflicts or grievances within the couple that are not being faced up to. Since this reason is usually present or even prevalent, I explain that these hidden difficulties have led to inner turmoil and unhappiness. They have not been explained, dealt with jointly in the marriage. Often this stems from the feeling of a shared unconscious obligation to have to adapt to the partner, to be always nice and agreeable, not to stir up trouble and to contribute to peace within the marriage and in the home. Of course it is good to be nice and agreeable, of course we should contribute to peace in the home, but when there is real difficulty it should be explained:

  Again, in case a circumstance causes a real offence between the two, they must not keep it in their hearts, but rather explain its nature to each other and try to remove it as soon as possible. ('Abdu'l-Bahá)[1]

- When people turn to a specialist for their sexual dysfunction, they usually have come to a stage of crisis and often believe their relationship has come to an end. It is useful to regard crisis in a different light: the beginning of change, of opening up, of acknowledging suffering, vulnerability, weaknesses, and each other's diversity, and of working toward a more encompassing level of unity and understanding. A crisis usually arises when a page of a large chapter in life is swiftly turning and a new stage is beckoning on the horizon − for example, the change from the carefree life of newly-weds to the one of expecting a first child, or the birth of subsequent children, or the stage when children leave home and sever the psychological cord.

- Belated emancipation in women usually opens the door for much friction, as no man is ready to give up his privileges without an honest fight!

- Depression, anxiety, frustration or the fact of feeling "burned out" are only symptoms veiling the real problems in individuals and their relationship. These symptoms should not be dwelled upon, as they can distort the underlying problem which will have to be tackled by both partners in a satisfactory way. Focusing only on the symptoms will detract attention from the problem and turn it on the "sick" person only. This leads to a dead end.

- Many women don't have a realistic or personal relationship with their own body. They either never became alive or have "gone dead", i.e. many intimate parts of their body are numb as if they had been anaesthetized. Very often a woman has never learnt to respect her body's needs and desires. She does not give ear to its positive expressions such as the need for tenderness, touch, and appreciation on the part of the partner, nor to its signals and warnings of limitations such as tiredness, or the need to be alone and not bothered or used. At a relatively late stage in life she will have to plunge into the abyss of her own needs and desires, get to know them and learn body language.

- Many men have never learned the vocabulary of tenderness and of respect for a woman.
- Most people have never been initiated into the methods of consultation, communication and cooperation, or to the notion of sexual equality. These notions and methods need to be learned. When unravelling the sexual dysfunction of a couple it is useful to fathom the different things the partners have learned: the unconscious attitudes, the non-verbal expression of prejudice and menacing information a child of tender age may have misinterpreted or understood literally. All of these have a lasting effect on people and mould their drives and their desires, accounting for part of the conflicts and difficulties that arise later on. It is evident that despite the bravura of "We know better, we've read up on all that, we don't follow our mothers and fathers", the antiquated, outdated injunctions of former generations are still working in people of today. Unfortunately for the sexual partners, sexual identity and the attitudes that tie up with it are mainly unconscious and stem from childhood; they are learned through example and not by word. These models change only slowly.
- Regretfully, many people only become aware at a late stage that they have been the victims of sexual abuse such as incest or abuse by friends or strangers. This experience can stultify the sexual potential of an individual.
- Usually, a couple have not learned to express emotions to one another in a manner understandable to both, and they become enmeshed in communication difficulties. Children are proficient in the field of communication of emotions as long as they have not learned to suppress their natural desire to communicate.
- Many women are awed by men's strength and aura of power, bodily and verbal. They have not learned to express their own values, opinions and vision of things verbally.

They lack the confidence to express their more emotional and sociable nature in the presence of men. Women have to learn to assume their nature and to express it with confidence, and verbally, when with men.

■ Often, a man and a woman who live together and have lived together for years do not know each other, not even physically. Thus, I quite often tell them something along the following lines: "Nature has made men more aggressive, more muscular. Their fathers and mothers educated them to become goal-oriented, extrovert, active and intense in what they undertake." This is so also the case in sexuality. A man usually likes a brief introduction, but does not want to dwell on the introduction. He then likes to feel the meat, that is the important part to him, between his teeth! The important part is what happens genitally; it is intense, active, with a rapid climax and a need for recuperation.

A woman has her sexuality spread over all of her body: her sexuality is in her skin, under her skin, and also genitally. It is global, not concentrated. She feels sexual with different variations of touch. Even gestures outside the bedroom, like receiving flowers, a touch, a warm look, make her feel "sexual" whereas this seldom is the case for a man. If this all-encompassing part of sexuality is very meagre or non-existent on the part of her partner, a women often is not "turned on". When aroused a woman can have a whole ripple of orgasms, one after another, which often is a source of astonishment to men.

This of course is a simplification, generalized and exaggerated, but very often rings a bell to both partners about different expectations and sensations.

■ In sexuality we're naked – inwardly, not only outwardly! There's no hiding who we are, but usually we do not realize this. A brutal man will be brutal sexually, a timid woman will be timid and passive, an imaginative person

7

will want to invent, a passionate one exudes passion — unless they are blocked.

As we are naked, we express emotions, not only the beautiful and human ones, but also the animal and dark-sided ones. In a way they escape our control. Thus, a woman who has kept her anger against her tyrannical father tightly locked up in her chest or her belly will express this hate against her man! A man whose mother was over-possessive and protective will want to wrench loose from this obsessive mother when making love with his wife — and his wife may not be overly possessive, but still gets a bucketful of anger every time they make love!

Sexual identity: A story of generations

Unforgettable was my encounter with a fifth-generation Bahá'í of Zoroastrian background. We had never met before and were never to meet again.

What she said as we chatted was confirmed for me while reading the short chapter on the Zoroastrians by John Huddleston in his book *The Search for a Just Society*:

No distinction is made between the souls of men and women, and consequently in the Zoroastrian Faith women have been treated more equitably than in most other cultures . . . [The Zoroastrians] are known for their higher than normal standards of education . . . high sexual morality (reputedly there is no such person as a Zoroastrian prostitute).[2]

Our conversation centred around the theme of sexual identity. This calm and impressive woman spoke of her belief that religion and its traditions profoundly mould what is termed sexual identity. Her dark eyes under a broad forehead had a serene look when she added:

"For sexual identity to change, I believe, it takes at least six generations after changing one's religion!"

Looking at her sagacious eyes and feminine form full of dignity, I thought that she and her family had achieved within their five generations what others from less fortunate backgrounds would have to labour over much longer! In her own way, full of assurance, this Bahá'í of Zoroastrian background expressed a reality: sexual identity is an important part of our identity; the fact of being conceived, born and educated a boy or a girl is an important part of our identity and may even tide over into afterlife. Learning and suffering are different for a man and a woman.

Sexual identity encompasses sexuality which in turn is more than sexual activity. Religion has profoundly determined sexual identity. Each religion has created models for man and woman, intimated the content of relationship between the sexes or even legislated upon it. Each religion, in its days of glory, has borne fairest fruit on the subject of sexual identity; in its long decadence, every religion has opened upon a dark abyss of vice, perversion, lust and emptiness.

The fairest fruit of the Bahá'í dispensation on the subject of sexual identity is the gift of equality to the sexes and the elevation of chastity as a personal quality for both sexes and the guarantor of happier marriages.

A story of apples

The Bahá'ís do not believe in the suppression of the sex impulse but in its regulation and control. (Shoghi Effendi).[3]

Some years ago Professor Hossain Danesh of Canada, introducing a round table on sexuality at a Conference for Bahá'í Studies on "Health and Healing" told the following story:

All through the ages parents have introduced the subject of sexuality to their growing children in the following vein: "Dear children, the world is beautiful and full of wonderful delights. There are trees and shrubs with delicious berries; there are peaches — peaches are juicy and sweet, taste the peaches and enjoy them. Then there are apricots, pears, plums and melons, so light, sweet and refreshing . . . you may taste all these delicious fruits! Then there are strawberries, raspberries, blueberries and the inviting blackberry, also the gooseberry – all these lovely fruits you may pick, eat and enjoy. There is only one fruit, dear children, which you should not taste, and you should shun these fruits and beware of them: apples!" And what happened all through the ages? All growing children, all youth, even all men and women in their mature age were thinking of nothing but apples! Thinking of forbidden apples!

This delightful story depicts the paradigm of sexuality and its inevitable influence on the thoughts and preoccupations, desires and inhibitions of people all through the ages, taking up so much of the private and intimate thoughts, feelings and desires of mankind, often to such a degree that people lost their balance and happiness, and went overboard on a wild chase for the chimera of sexual happiness. The outcome can well be what Shoghi Effendi, Guardian of the Bahá'í Faith, put so beautifully into words:

We often feel that our happiness lies in a certain direction; and yet, if we have to pay too heavy a price for it in the end we may discover that we have not really purchased either freedom or happiness, but just some new situation of frustration and disillusion.

When I was training as a psychiatrist, a colleague and I drove up to a mountain village. I was driving, and we were going to visit a family of clients. Somehow conversation turned in such a way that we spoke about sexuality and I ventured to say that my religion, the Bahá'í Faith, had a positive outlook on sexuality and regarded it as the "natural right of every individual", and that thus there was practically no room, in a healthy Bahá'í family, for the guilt feelings associated with the suppression of an individual's sexual desires in a neurotic form. My colleague asked a few questions and then we came to speak of other matters. After our visit my colleague abruptly said:

"I shall be taking the train and shall not be going back with you by car."

I was so surprised by this that I had to park the car by the side of the road to think about what had happened. I realized that this man, a Freudian by conviction and training, had been totally appalled and unsettled in his beliefs on hearing that a religion had such a positive outlook on sexuality! In a way, I made out, his "Weltbild" (view of the world) had been seriously challenged.

Most people, I presume, have made up their "Weltbild" on the assumption of a warped outlook on sexuality stemming from the decline of religion as a healthy and positive force, and on the other hand are battling with a haze of insecure knowledge and precepts concerning this important, but not all-important, matter. Most people I have met in my life have carefully hidden difficulties of a sexual and erotic nature: their model is so warped! No healthy sexuality with a warped model!

Worse, most people spend great parts of their life suppressing their sexuality, fighting their sexuality, hiding their sexuality and their feelings – because it is not directed through a pure and healthy channel!

But this standard of ours will produce healthier, happier, nobler people, and induce stabler marriages. (Shoghi Effendi)[4]

2

Traditional attitudes looming over the present

"The head of the woman is the man", wrote St. Paul, ". . . neither was the man created for the woman; but the woman for the man."[1] The authority of St. Paul (not Jesus) has defined relationships between men and women throughout Christendom for two thousand years, and the model is still very much with us, as witness the continuing uproar caused by the ordination of women to the priesthood. "I suffer not a woman to teach, nor to usurp authority over the man, but to be in silence," was the advice of St. Paul.[2]

Most women stemming from the Christian culture are moving away from this paradigm, but sadly, they still find themselves enmeshed in an antiquated system of relationships within the family and most of all the couple. A whole palette of different attitudes can be observed. Revolt is part of the phenomenon of breaking loose from the old model: it can be open or hidden, active or passive, but practically all women are struggling in some way to free themselves. In consequence, all men are plunged into the struggle too, as to their way of thinking they are having to lose old privileges and prerogatives . . .

Here are two couples who have remained in the old model. The woman's attitude is passive in one case, active in the other, but neither of them have been able to deal positively with the problem; both are despondent.

Maggie is the always submissive, silently sighing wife of a peremptory man; she has sunk into severe alcoholism over the years. When her husband feels lonely at night, he "uses" her even though she's asleep.

Maria, coming from a Mediterranean culture, has plenty of temperament to rant about her husband — both to the many doctors she visits and to her three sons. She is a lonely, tortured woman who often lies in bed nursing her many real and imaginary ills. The weekend, she feels, should not exist — it is then that her husband, a primitive man who gets bored when he's not at work, uses her intensely for his own relief. Her revolt comes out during the week when she raves at him — but only when talking to her doctors and her sons . . .

Some women love the traditional role when their children are small, but slip into revolt once the children become independent of their care. This can often end in tragedy, as in the case of Josie and Ted.

Josie was the good-natured, not too intelligent wife of Ted, whose job as a train-driver had made him obsessive about order, punctuality and a well-run household. They were in deep trouble: Josie had fallen in love with a man of light morality who kept her dangling at his beck and call. He was a real charmer who knew how to play with her feelings. The more Ted remonstrated, the more infatuated Josie became — as light-hearted as a teenager, forgetting the well-being of Ted and their two children. There seemed to be no way out, and in the end Ted became determined to divorce Josie.

With Ted and Josie, a very common pattern had become full-blown, and it was a disaster for the whole family. Both of them were convinced of the sacredness and rightness of the traditional roles: man is superior to woman and thus must guide her, dominate her, keep her within bounds, etc. Busy with romantic love, then home-making and child-care, they woke up to their plight only when their children were nearly grown up and their eldest had fallen in love — so much so that she was willing to leave home, family and friends to follow her man to the other end of the earth! History repeats itself . . .

Only then did Josie realize, deep down, that she had given all of twenty years of her life to her man unconditionally, and that she had abandoned her job training for his sake – he was older and wanted a home (and a homemaker) without having to support his wife through her apprenticeship. Worse, she had not grown an inch as a person. She had, though, fulfilled all her social roles to perfection, as spouse, homemaker and most of all mother: Ted had had no reproaches to make until the unhappy incident of Josie's affair. As for Ted, he too had been irreproachable: faithful, supportive of his family and of his in-laws, unconditionally and sacrificially.

Pleasure-loving, not given to reflection, and shying away from any pain or suffering, Josie plunged headlong into her new romance, but was still deeply attached to her husband and continued to live with him. She was not willing to suffer, reflect and grow; to search for new principles further afield to give her the necessary perspective to order her life anew. She had no faith in her religion (whose principles as to the relationship of man and woman she followed to the letter, but without the elements of true love, loyalty and faithfulness). Thus, she exchanged one condition for another very similar one: being the servant and admirer of a man of whom she expected all the bliss in the world. When her affair began to become threadbare she still would not stop to think. She continued with the see-saw between the two men, liking the game of being the cherished, sought-after prize of each of them. Only – neither of the men would go on with the game! Her husband thought of divorce, her lover turned more and more to his former steady girlfriend. Josie's affair, very much based on romanticism, was not such a happy one sexually, but she glossed over this fact with unrealistic hopes and flushes of excitement.

Immersed in materialism and guided only by tradition, Ted and Josie are heading for tragedy.

Other women have more courage and faith in evolution and are determined to work towards a model of responsibility and consciousness, as the equal counterpart of a man. They decide to work patiently to bring about more traits of this new model, aware that after thousands of years of the old ways, the new model isn't just going to happen by itself. They have to pass through trial and suffering, and to all outward seeming their relationships don't look very good. They have very evident difficulties and have to struggle for a very long time — often for years!

Stemming from different backgrounds and having learned early that life is hazardous, Robert and Mary became friends and married young. Their characters and outlook were still flexible and they were not afraid of changing their habits or character traits to achieve more intimacy. When Robert was under severe stress at work for a time, and Mary was much absorbed by three little children, they tried not to sever their tie. They took time to reflect and consult over their weakening relationship and the lessening of their sexual ardour. This was hard and painful work. Sometimes they felt like giving up, but something told them to persevere. Also, they had a firm hold on moral principles and faith; they wanted to abide by the principles of loyalty and faithfulness, and to pray, even though love was not always felt as a warm glow, but more as perseverance. With time, they felt more at ease with this new phase of their lives, and unimagined resources came to their rescue to strengthen their relationship. Their sex life followed the new zest in the relationship.

Still other couples, preferring to grow, and unable to muster the strength to face their relationship and sexuality, silently renounce both sexuality and the relationship, but grow as individuals. Mariana and John, for instance, are devoted to a common cause. First it was raising their family and working side by side for the community. Then, as the children went off first to school and then to university, they both flung themselves sacrificially into the arms of encompassing neverending tasks. In their life together each of them tried to fulfil the expectations of the other as to role-functioning, but felt at a loss to mend or even develop the relationship. Chins up, they lived the lives of suffering saints and heroes. Their sexual life was sorely amiss, but they learned to bear with it.

Sexual life, it seems, flows naturally if the relationship is an evolving one, and if people are willing to grow and accept the pain of growth. Sexual life is not independent of people's principles or beliefs. Most of all, it cannot be satisfying if there is underlying war! Nor can it be satisfying if there is a refusal to grow, both individually and in the relationship, in accordance with the never-ending flow of life. When a chapter of family life closes, for instance when children are ready to leave home, a couple should review their relationship and their personal lives, and be ready to alter things.

Josie, for instance, was counselled to reopen the chapter of learning and job training, to find out how she could learn new job skills and thereby gain more self-esteem and confidence. Ted, it was suggested, should learn how to be a partner to a modern woman – support her in her own projects so that she could develop, and take more initiative himself for planning their time together. (He had always left all this to Josie, concentrating solely on his job and personal well-being.)

When people refuse to grow, they revert to former stages and their methods, thus closing off their potential. Josie reverted to falling for a man and giving him everything, in exchange (she hoped) for bliss. Ted would not outgrow his habit of handing over responsibility for his well-being to a woman.

It seems that the old adage "You can't have your cake and eat it too" is still true: without growth and the necessary pain, you cannot experience joy. In other words, happiness is a quickly vanishing commodity unless it is sustained by spiritual (that is, durable) foundations.

This is not a popular notion among those who see sexuality as a matter-of-fact accompaniment to life and a source of never-ending pleasure. This view is so prevalent that it is very difficult, without a new philosophy of spiritually-based growth and relationship, to move into this very new chapter of equality in relationships between man and woman:

The world today is submerged, amongst other things, in an over-exaggeration of the importance of physical love, and a dearth of spiritual values.[3]

. . . The soul who steadfastly obeys the law of Bahá'u'lláh, however hard it may seem, grows spiritually, while the one who compromises with the law for the sake of his own apparent happiness is seen to have been following a chimera: he does not gain the happiness he sought, he retards his spiritual advance and often brings new problems upon himself.[4]

"The man in my life"

"He for God only, she for God in him." Milton's immortal lines gave emphasis to St. Paul for centuries throughout the English-speaking world. But according to the Bahá'í teachings, the paradigm has changed:

Verily God created women for men, and men for women. (Bahá'u'lláh)[5]

The world of humanity consists of two parts: male and female. Each is the complement of the other. Therefore, if one is defective, the other will necessarily be incomplete, and perfection cannot be attained. ('Abdu'l-Bahá)[6]

What used to be the only right way to proceed for a woman, i.e. to build her life around a man, is now becoming disastrous in its consequences. The destructive mechanisms of this old model are becoming more and more apparent.

One young woman had been a "model child", although thoughtful and rebellious deep down. Her father adored her, but he would have preferred a boy. She did her best to please her father, becoming a tomboy, accompanying him on fishing trips and even to political meetings. She was most unhappy when puberty began and her psyche and body underwent the normal major changes. She began to hide her breasts in voluminous pullovers, and avoided sport and family gatherings. By this time, father at long last had a baby boy to add to his girls and didn't necessarily mourn the change in his little daughter. When she wanted to learn a profession her father said, "Girls get married, they don't need professions." So she just had a job and then married as her mother and older sisters had done. When her two boys were 8 and 12 she woke up to a very unhappy situation: she felt she had married the wrong man, and also felt empty because of having no outlet to her creative faculties.

She became profoundly depressed and suicidal.

This woman had followed Daddy's instructions and had lived to please him; had followed Mummy's example – but found herself in a disastrous state of mind. She had built her life first around her father, then around her husband, and had done everything to educate her boys correctly. In the end her marriage came to the brink of a total breakdown, her husband refusing to accept sexual abstinence. She had no desire for sexual activity. When she came to think of it, she had never had any desire for sex. She had just gone along with it, as it was supposed to be part of married life.

Woman's lack of progress and proficiency has been due to her need of equal education and opportunity. Had she been allowed this equality, there is no doubt that she would be the counterpart of man in ability and capacity. The happiness of mankind will be realized when women and men coordinate and advance equally, for each is the complement and helpmeet of the other. ('Abdu'l-Bahá)[7]

After a year's therapy, in which her husband had at last agreed to participate, both partners acknowledged that they would not go back to the previous state of their marriage. But change was very painful, for their models of the marital relationship and of the roles of man and woman in life were so very tenacious. Such ideas imprisoned them in unhappy mechanisms of fault-finding and general discontent when things didn't follow the age-old patterns set for man and woman.

Another woman, a girl of twenty, had two affairs, but each time she shied away from becoming committed and having to face the pain in herself and the difficulties in the relationship. She liked each of the young men and had no major reproach, but, she admitted, something in her own self made her recoil and break off the relationship, despite a lot of regret and sadness afterwards. She realized that at the roots of her difficulty was the incapacity to find a model of relationship to a man which would be different from the highly immature relationship of her parents. She had suffered so much from it — father egotistical and tyrannical, mother egocentric and childish, both of them enmeshed in a form of relationship where women seemingly sacrifice everything but become more and more empty, whereas men become brutal in spite of themselves.

Divine Justice demands that the rights of both sexes should be equally respected since neither is superior to the other in the eyes of Heaven. Dignity before God depends, not on sex, but on purity and luminosity of heart. Human virtues belong equally to all! ('Abdu'l-Bahá)[8]

3

Qualities and attitudes necessary in a relationship of equality

IN a relationship of equality, friendship, respect and esteem rank highest. These are the qualities which build the foundations of true love, as opposed to infatuation.

Through these qualities a couple do not become enmeshed in a romantic relationship which must necessarily lead to disillusionment, disappointment and heartbreak.

A couple, then, are looking in the same direction, as Saint-Exupéry said, not into each other's infatuated eyes. To look in the same direction is necessary and indispensable for two people setting out to face life with the intention of mastering its hazards, difficulties and hardships, and wanting to overcome the suffering that goes with living.

It is thus important, in a relationship of equality, to have certain common fields of interest, concern and endeavour, be it in the community, in the family and neighborhood, in art or science or business or any other field. But in the last resort even this is not sufficient. The partners have to lay a firm spiritual foundation. This is the only means of purifying them and their relationship and permitting them to overcome tests. In the end, the only guarantor for a relationship is the faith that God will protect it. This faith has to be nourished daily!

But thou must submit to and rely upon God under all conditions and He will bestow upon thee that which is conducive to thy well-being. Verily He is the merciful and compassionate! For how many an affair was involved in difficulty and then was straightened, and how many a problem was solved by the permission of God. ('Abdu'l-Bahá)[1]

The word "love" is very much misused today. The abuse of such an important concept empties it of meaning. Thus, it may be wise, at a time of general uneasiness and doubt, to describe certain aspects of love, particularly those that are important in building a durable foundation for a relationship.

Reciprocity

In former times, reciprocity in the marital relationship was a rarity, as women were very much viewed as pieces of property or even considered as animals.

A man was free either to use his donkey with kindness or until the donkey broke down and died under unfair treatment. Today, in the industrialized world, a man has the same choice about his car: he can either treat it with consideration of its needs and knowledge of its mechanics, or he can ride it onto the scrap-heap without ever paying attention to its need for servicing, changes of oil or spare parts. A woman can clean and tend her sewing machine or computer, or misuse it until it is blocked and worthless. Even a spoon or a knife can either be kept clean and in order, or else allowed to rust or become tarnished.

In an age where the tendency is to treat human beings in the same way as machines, it is not easy to come to a true understanding of human nature and the laws governing relationships, even if our goal is happiness, harmony and growth of the individual, of relationships and of society.

In this day and age when women are learning for the first time that human dignity applies to them too, it is of absolute importance for men to learn about the laws of reciprocity and not expect a woman to serve without recompense, not to impose on a woman what she does not want. Today it is important for both men and women to begin asking their spouses about their likes and dislikes, so they can get to know them as human beings with individual characteristics. This applies to the marital relationship in spirit, mind and feelings, and also of course to the physical bond. It is necessary to get to know the individual beliefs, the individual likes and idiosyncrasies without embarking necessarily on a conquest of the person or a crusade to change that person's standards.

This basic law of reciprocity is often not respected in any way in society as a whole, not only between men and women. But the great art of hiding truth through a profusion of words and the fervid profession of sincerity of motive, again through words, often obscures the hideous fact that there is little reciprocity in our present-day life.

But sexuality is a true barometer of reciprocity! Sexuality is a bodily expression of many spiritual principles, among them reciprocity.

The law of reciprocity is similar to fairness and justice: if it is appropriate for you to receive, then I also may receive. If you want to express what you feel, would it not be fair for me to be able to express what I feel too? If you have a right to fulfil your wants and desires, would it not be proper for me to find a response to mine? If, one day, I have no desire or need, would it not be appropriate for you accept this, since it seems that you take it for granted that sometimes you are busy, preoccupied, tired or absent? If sometimes your love expresses itself in a quiet way, and at other times in a tender, or a more fiery and passionate mode, would it not be possible for you to imagine that I also go through these various shades of needs and moods without wanting to offend or reject you – is this not reciprocity?

When the law of reciprocity is systematically suppressed

and there is no respect of it in one or in both partners, sexuality, like a channel of water, gets clogged up: there may be just a trickle going from the one to the other, but not in the other direction! Then people become worried, angry or perplexed – and they resort to the common explanation: my partner, you know, is depressed – we must get some treatment for him or her. When she's had some treatment for her depression things will go back to normal!

"Darling! You look wonderful!"

Who wouldn't want to hear this from their spouse? But tragically, for many women it can mean that her partner only wants to see the good, healthy, "always there" side of his "woman". The wife then feels that she has to repress her tiredness, her sadness, her disappointments or lack of enthusiasm, and try always to look "wonderful".

What happens when a couple functions like this, or the women of a household feel they owe this to the men?

Some time ago one of my colleagues referred a Spanish woman to me who had gone through two cancer operations and was nearly crazy with the anxiety of it all. She had had a very hard-working life, but had enjoyed being the one who was able to carry everything on her shoulders – in fact her husband, her sons, her employer and her father had always relied on her for moral strength. Then her strength broke down and she had cancer – and then the immense sadness welled up in seas of tears, endless tears. Her husband told her, "It isn't good for you to cry, you shouldn't cry."

I had the good lady explain to her husband that she had a subterranean lake of sadness and if he let her cry without remonstrating with her she would get better. He complied; she cried for three weeks and then didn't cry any more.

When sadness or tiredness or any other natural emotion is repressed for a long time, it creates havoc in the mind, the soul and body of a person. And many men cannot really face these natural manifestations in their female companions. (Although it seems natural to *them* to express tiredness or disenchantment or want of zeal freely, looking for the corresponding consolation and understanding from their wives.) As a French writer puts it: "Nothing contrasts more sharply with the masculine image of self-confidence, rationality and control, than men's sulky, obtuse and often virtually total dependence on their wives to articulate and deal with their own unhappy feelings, and their own insensitivity, fear and passivity in helping their wives to deal with theirs." (Marc Feigen Fasteau). It is worth saying that that was written by a man.

Women are often not allowed to express their sadness (a sad woman is not a good companion, so to say!), tiredness or disappointment; they then repress it, but often these natural emotions come out under cover of different facades – anger, or hurt silence. Men too are traditionally not allowed to express sadness by weeping, or showing a sad face – they have to become irritable, angry or even violent instead!

Little have we learned to listen to such quietly ticking laws as the one of reciprocity. All of us like fair play and justice, both in our own affairs and in the law of society!

In several Western countries the courts have recently – and for the first time in history – ruled that a woman must not be subjected to sexual intercourse against her will, even if she is married. This is a great stride forward in the direction of the law of reciprocity for both sexes.

In modern sexology, when a couple's sexual relationship has broken down due to some symptom expressing suffering (impotence in the man or frigidity in the woman, or the absence of a normal need for sexual activity), one begins treatment by teaching them to find out each other's bodily needs through to caressing. Man and woman have to find this out and help their partner become aware of their needs. This is a good measure of the couple's capacity to learn the law of reciprocity, apart from learning tenderness in a physical sense.

Respect

Mutual respect is a very important spiritual attitude in a marital relationship and, of course, affects the physical bond.

Love is not complete if it does not comprise respect, for respect teaches us to consider the individuality, the likes and dislikes, the beliefs, attitudes and standards of our spouse. Mutual respect is important, as no one in his right senses really feels loved if there is no respect coming from the partner. No one can truly love a person without giving true consideration to that person's individuality and appreciating and valuing it as something precious and unique.

Often people (and I'm sorry to say it is often the man) pretend they love their spouse, but have no idea that respect is part of love, and unhappily the spouse with time understands this sorry state of affairs. Then love transforms itself into sadness and depression, because there is a realization that this passionate love really is possessive and selfish, and does not comprise respect and appreciation of the otherness of the spouse.

Respect makes it impossible for a person to force a partner or to impose upon him or her. As respect grows in our heart we understand the qualities of our spouse as a person and thus would not want to impose or force this person to do anything he would not want to do of his own free will.

When mutual respect is growing in the hearts and minds of partners, their relationship is permeated by a realization of freedom and love, and this forms a firm bond. This freedom, of course, is not freedom in the sense of infidelity, but freedom of the spirit and the mind.

Friendship

. . . will be his friend throughout all his life . . . ('Abdu'l-Bahá)[2]
Their purpose must be this: to become loving companions and comrades and at one with each other for time and eternity . . . mutual attachment of mind and heart. ('Abdu'l-Bahá)[3]

At present new chapters of learning await couples in the way of friendship.

Friendship has been an ideal for many centuries, but in practice has been possible only for the élite. It exists in songs and poems, in novels, essays, philosophy, plays and the great myths of past civilizations. But historically, friendships seem to have been few and far between. The common man and woman had no time for friendship, neither in marriage nor elsewhere: life was busy and wore people out.

In many societies, though, friendship began to be cultivated by men in a rudimentary way, particularly when the women were not around. Hence the nostalgia for the type of bonding that occurs in war, between soldiers or, more mundanely, on the sports ground and in the pub. Women, on the other hand, were kept busy. Cultivating friendship was just not feasible.

Friendship has become an essential bonding mechanism, in a time when marital crisis in all societies is glaring. The lack of true friendship between marriage partners is one of the reasons marriages go stale, peter off into unfaithfulness, break up in a crisis or wither slowly. When a marriage is in a crisis, friendship is one of the most healing remedies.

Such a crisis often comes as the couple passes from one stage to another.

In the beginning, instinct, passion, sensuality and role-thinking are important bonding mechanisms between people. They are not, it goes without saying, sufficient to maintain the bond. As time passes and the relationship is subjected to tension and stress from all sides — personal and social — friendship becomes essential to strengthen the relationship against the forces that are tending to undermine it. Friendship also constitutes a refuge in times of stress or unhappiness.

Should people not have developed a strong friendship they will rapidly be engulfed in traditional patterns of role-thinking. They may fall back on their family of origin or their old cronies instead of turning to the life-companion and the aims of this new phase. Family and old friends will reclaim them all too gladly and prevent them from bonding in a significant way. Friendship is a very strong bonding force against such pervasive and all-too-natural influences. In adverse circumstances, the newly-weds and lovers may become encompassed again in family strife (strife is an excellent means of reclaiming a stray family member!) and old habits can become overpowering if the tie of friendship between the partners has not grown to be a stronger force of attraction.

In the next stage, the one of parenting small children, friendship is most needed. This is when a mother tends to become isolated from the outside world and a father often feels cut off from his wife because of the overpowering need of his offspring. Now it is essential to remain aware of the great need of both partners to maintain a deep and friendly relationship, so that they will not be torn apart through the needs of offspring or jobs and fall into old patterns of role-thinking and separateness.

As the children grow older and enter puberty and adolescence the necessity for friendship in a couple becomes even more evident. During this stage of the family many couples become aware of an immense gap in their relationship which can very often be spelled out as an absence of friendship. Thus it is important to maintain and consciously deepen friendship as the children grow. During the children's adolescence, the prevalent tendency for couples to separate and divorce will exert a powerful influence.

When children leave their parents, and they are left to restructure their lives as a couple preparing for old age, friendship is a most precious bond, for it allows them to review all aspects of their lives and to introduce new chapters into their relationship. Being aware of the necessity of friendship and of course of their underlying loyalty to each other, a couple will then be able to maintain and deepen their bond and acquire new depths and spirituality.

Likewise, if people remain in crisis and are not able to recreate a vital and healthy bond, friendship has not been integrated into their relationship. They have had too little to share, they are worlds apart, and have not made the necessary effort to cultivate the few things they did share. Both of them have remained "tyrants", i.e. they want the other to join them in their interests, hobbies or passions, but have not learned the art of acquiring new interests merely for love of a person and the relationship. Many people like to stay in their shell, like an oyster, too afraid to open up and experience a different world. Two oysters certainly share very little!

Friendship allows the partner to appreciate the personal sides of the life-companion, and not only the social or sexual role. Men tend to appreciate the good cook, the perfect housewife and devoted mother and spouse in their wives: these are the social roles. Women have a tradition of appreciating the security, protection and prestige their man offers them. Is this enough in an age where social roles are becoming less clear-cut and so many men are good cooks, perfect house-husbands and admirable fathers? Likewise, is it enough for a woman who earns, receives appreciation in her job or career and has enough personality to take a stand on her own to have a husband who appreciates her chiefly for her housekeeping? It is precisely in our modern times that we need new bonding qualities and mechanisms. Friendship is one of these – and it is essential!

Thus, a man should be expected to see the personal qualities in his wife and to appreciate and value them. A wife should value her life-companion for his personality (in a positive sense) and thus make a friend of him. Character traits, qualities, human skills, faculties, potential, and also spiritual ideals, values and aspirations become the stuff of friendship.

Beyond the marital relationship, friendship will open up entirely new paths for both men and women, particularly if jealousy and possessiveness are stowed away for ever and provided they learn to value their spouse's faculty of forming pure and spiritual friendships with persons of either sex.

. . . that they may strive with all their might until universal fellowship, close and warm, and unalloyed love, and spiritual relationships, will connect all the hearts in the world . . . ('Abdu'l-Bahá)[4]

Loyalty

Loyalty is the quality that cemented a bond between noblemen and their king, between yeomen and their lord, between members of a clan.

Loyalty also is what used to make a captain want to sink with his ship, feeling so tied by honour and responsibility to the ship and his duty that he would rather give up his life than abandon them.

According to 'Abdu'l-Bahá, loyalty is an essential quality for maintaining the marriage bond. It is a very spiritual quality that will "unite the hearts" ('Abdu'l-Bahá),[5] and is thus capable of maintaining important bonds for the great tasks in life. It is an essential part of a contract, and marriage can certainly be termed a contract – for life and even beyond, if the intention in the marriage is a spiritual one.

Eva was married under rather unhappy circumstances to Walter. She never felt happy in their marriage, but had a great sense of loyalty and this was reciprocated by Walter. Loyalty was at certain times the only quality that held them together, for many destructive forces were at work in their relationship, including cultural and intellectual differences. Unfortunately they were not good communicators or else they would have discussed their very firm, but rigid, bond of loyalty and come to more flexible attitudes that would have allowed them to have a more loving and friendly relationship. Loyalty kept them together until death; they did have a recompense in a way, for their relationship became more spiritual and mellowed in the last weeks of their lives.

Loyalty is a particularly important quality when positive feelings such as love, amity, and affection have drained out of the relationship in a transient or a permanent way. Loyalty then maintains the bond even in the face of disaster.

Life cannot always be amenable, and thus it is important that basic qualities such as loyalty should be woven into the marital bond. The quality we term loyalty is one of those that brings out the "metal" of personalities, and of relationships; it is capable of maintaining the relationship in spite of great hardship.

Chastity

All the great religions teach chastity and commend it as a virtue. However, it is a virtue that has fallen into disrepute in the permissive society of the last twenty-five years. Nowadays, partly in response to the AIDS epidemic and also, perhaps, because the wheel has come full circle, chastity is beginning to be taken seriously again the Western world.

This, to many parents, sounds good in principle and as a wholesome theory. Chastity may even have been upheld by them in their instructions to their growing children. It is also upheld in books on saints and biographies of people of great purity. Such books may be on bookshelves – but are they read today?

One of the difficulties is that, in practice, society has followed a double standard for men and women. Men, by and large, were regarded as free to roam and to conquer women, and thus were not only allowed but encouraged to "get experience" and know whom to "choose" if marriage was thought of as a goal. The chosen, though, would have to be pure and chaste.

Women were supposed to stay pure, even naive, except for

those who broke the standard and joined men in conquest and play – but these were not the sort of woman a man should marry!

Thus, boys received instructions on how to conquer women. Helped by father, mother, brothers, sisters and friends in the great game to prove their worth as men (this game being devoid of feeling for the person "conquered"), boys came under pressure through the rivalry of their peers and the necessity of proving their so-called virility. Girls, on the other hand, were supposed to be subdued in their perceptions of eroticism, and were controlled and subjugated by instructions on how to keep pure and safeguard themselves from male lust. Fathers, mothers, sisters, brothers and friends once again joined in this counter-balancing effort.

This double standard in education – which is of course a logical impossibility – has built up into individual and social neurosis (maladaptation to reality) culminating either in stark degeneration – homosexuality, refusal and inability to commit oneself to marriage and family, morbid states of neurosis, depression and anxiety – or in flat refusal to comply, thus breaking with tradition and often going against parents' wishes, in search of a new standard and a new concept better adapted to modern-day reality.

The consequence of the double standard today, apart from its profound influence on society, is a distortion of character in the lives of individuals:

■ Women eventually revolt against an unjust practice. They end up either in open mutiny, thus incapacitating their development in society and as a partner, venting their grievances and consequently having to face the harsh reactions of many people, both in their families and among men in general. Or they suppress their revolt against the injustice, but become depressed or tortured by the split

between inner revolt and outward submission, which often maims their character for life.
- Men develop a harsh and superior attitude to the other sex, and in the end become insensitive not only towards women but towards life in general — towards the suffering, the destitute, the poor, the victims of oppression, or those in trial and despair.

Where can we find values which will heal this state of affairs and answer modern-day needs?

In the Bahá'í teachings, chastity

implies both before and after marriage an unsullied, chaste sex life. Before marriage absolutely chaste, after marriage absolutely faithful to one's chosen companion. Faithful in all sexual acts, faithful in word and in deed.[6]

Moreover, for Bahá'ís chastity applies to both men and women:

Say: He is not to be numbered with the people of Bahá who followeth his mundane desires, or fixeth his heart on things of the earth . . . if he met the fairest and most comely of women, he would not feel his heart seduced by the least shadow of desire for her beauty. Such an one, indeed, is the creation of spotless chastity. Thus instructeth you the Pen of the Ancient of Days, as bidden by your Lord, the Almighty, the All-Bountiful. (Bahá'u'lláh)[7]

Chastity, or purity, in the erotic and sexual life of individuals and society is "one of the most challenging concepts to get across in this very permissive age" says the Universal House of Justice in a letter written in 1985. It challenges history and the adaptation by most societies of their religious and spiritual values to routine and everyday life. It challenges the ingrained values, attitudes and habits of men and women everywhere, high and low! This challenge is like a plough slowly furrowing the land and bringing rich, pure soil to the surface to be cultivated by new generations and societies.

In a new society where both boys and girls, men and women practise chastity before and within wedlock, each sex will have a profound sense of justice and will be freed of disastrous consequences in their lives and characters.

Chastity, in this sense, is a life- and society-saving divine measure, although difficult to put into practice for people whose background is a society ably wielding the double standard. Through this vision, though, Bahá'ís the world over are joyously making efforts to uphold this new value and to hand it over to their children as a boon for the generations to come. In this way new foundations for society will slowly be raised and will yield the fruits of happier marriages.

Chastity has profound implications for the implementation of the equality of men and women announced by Bahá'u'lláh over a hundred years ago.

For millennia, chastity has been regarded as a kind of trump-card for women. They have adopted it as a life-saving protection when faced with a world full of brutality, abuse and sexual harassment, both physical and psychological. Thus, chastity has been used by women, often on the unconscious level, as a measure of protection not only from brutality and lust, but also of their own fragility when facing their own needs or potential. Fear of men, of their overpowering strength and potential brutality, has kept women in the home:

The status of woman in former times was exceedingly deplorable . . . If she pursued educational courses, it was deemed contrary to chastity; hence women were made prisoners of the household . . . Bahá'u'lláh destroyed these ideas and proclaimed the equality of man and woman. He made woman respected by commanding that all women be educated, that there be no difference in the education of the two sexes and that man and woman share the same rights. In the estimation of God there is no distinction of sex. ('Abdu'l-Bahá)[8]

To women, then, chastity was not only the guarantor of their virtue, but often of their lives, both in the home and outside: had they not clung to it, they would have been even more brutalized by their men. Had the fear of losing their virginity not kept them within bounds, in the home, in the family, they would have been brutalized, raped and destroyed outside of the home. Without any doubt it has "enslaved" them and their potential within the narrow bounds of the home.

Conversely, the enforcement of the law of chastity on women, both as a marketable virtue and a guarantor of their very life, has contributed to their being protected, to some degree, from degradation and perversity. Consequently they have been able to channel their aspirations towards the acquisition of those qualities in which women now excel: love, service, intuition, an alert mind and a sense of leadership and indomitable courage when confronted with danger.

What advantages will chastity bring men? A chaste character will permit them to abandon the age-old game of domination over women and the degrading habit of sexual boasting. These games will be gradually abandoned by the generality of men as they enter adulthood. This prize will permit men to acquire not only depth of character, but also of feelings, a thing that has not been seen as yet as a general trend.

Chastity in youth has special significance, both to preserve that great purity and strength characteristic of youth, and also to contain the strong desires and emotions that well up at this time. Great emotion, if spilled too rapidly and without being adequately channelled, will be a major destructive force in the life of a young person.

Such is the case if a pre-youth, say 13 or 14 years old, falls head over heels in love and decides then and there to share emotions, desire, needs, time, home and space with another person.

Should this great urge not be taken into account by, first of all, a low age limit for marriage (as is the case in the Bahá'í Faith, where people are allowed to marry at 15 provided the law of the land allows it); secondly, by reason (i.e. the necessity to look at aspects of reality, not only of emotion and desire); and most of all by the strengthening law of chastity, this person most probably will spend him- or herself and be consumed emotionally. Very little energy will be left to structure life from there on. This happens when young people are so unhappy in their parents' home that marrying or going to live with a member of the other sex seems the only viable alternative. These young people feel – often rightly – that if they stay in an unhealthy home they will become totally depressed and despairing. The answer then would be chastity, and also looking at reality and consulting with a body of responsible people to find a more viable alternative.

Chastity, then, is an energy-saving and channelling virtue, able to contain strong desire and emotions, and permitting methods such as reflection and consultation which will help the person concerned to take a firmer grip on reality and put necessary changes into action.

Chastity and purity of heart, soul and body go together. Chastity is an attitude that also guides a person to choose a partner: in this sense it is a protection for both men and women.

Chastity is not only the golden rule for individual sexual activity. It is also one of the qualities "so fundamental to the healthy functioning of human society that (it) must be upheld whatever the circumstances".[9] This sentence penned by the Universal House of Justice in one of its significant letters addressed to a physician speaks about the generality of laws that are of fundamental value for human society.

Without chastity, the evolution of human society is halted. Society then sinks into decadence and has to go through a long period of renewal, as happened after the fall of the Roman Empire. The fairest fruits of society – a civilization which expresses such aspects as justice, evolution, development, freedom within limits, culture – are impossible in a society which tramples the law of chastity underfoot.

Thus Bahá'ís, committed as they are to the fundamental progress of society, will make efforts in their own private lives to uphold this law so vital to the health of society.

As we have already seen, chastity has been an important aspect of all religions. Their founders have given a perfect example of this outstanding virtue, although this has often been misinterpreted both by followers and enemies. In Christianity, for example, Jesus' celibacy due to his homelessness has been interpreted as an ideal of abstinence and asceticism and incorporated into the rules of monasticism and priesthood.

The Bahá'í dispensation elevates the rank of chastity to a consciously practised virtue and discipline, and this seems to be one of its many novel aspects.

Also, the Bahá'í Writings speak of the purifying aspect of chastity, beyond the physical one in the sexual sphere: the purification of desire and the evolution towards detachment, the purity of feelings and ideas. If practised for generations, this vision of chastity will elevate individuals to new heights of strength (purity and strength are related) and thus bring forth people with new dimensions of virility and femininity:

. . . when the soul of man is exalted and his body but the tool for his enlightened spirit. (Shoghi Effendi)[10]

Concerning the positive aspects of chastity, Shoghi Effendi also states that the Bahá'í Faith recognizes the value of the sex impulse and holds that the institution of marriage has been established as the channel of its rightful expression. Bahá'ís do not believe that the sex impulse should be suppressed but that it should be regulated and controlled.[11]

Human beings will evolve both individually and collectively: the practice of chastity by both sexes will create a protection for individuals and society as yet never experienced in the history of mankind. It will strengthen people's character, their sense of responsibility for other people's intimate character, feelings and bodily impressions. Nobody will feel the right to transgress another person's intimacy without permission. People will, and this is the positive side of the coin, also be much more conscious in their sensations and enjoyment, and thus will not be carried away by their instincts and so become degraded.

Chastity in no way implies withdrawel from human relationships. It liberates people from the tyranny of the ubiquity of sex. A person who is in control of his sexual impulses is enabled to have profound and enduring friendships with many people, both men and women, without ever sullying that unique and priceless bond that should unite man and wife.[12]

In this sense chastity is an opening to new conquests of the human being and society at large: it permits people to associate, for the first time in history, without suspicion of any irregularity of an erotic or sexual nature. People will no longer need to be suspicious or jealous when they see their father or mother, brother or sister, husband or wife, son or daughter associating with a member of the opposite sex. This will construct a totally new network of relationships in human society. This phenomenon, now in its birth-pangs, but sorely hampered by the non-practice of chastity, will be released from its fetters when people adhere to chastity and stop the game of suspicion, jealousy, envy, etc. For these childish methods have helped to imprison women in the home!

All divine laws, in a sense, have the role of protecting human beings from stepping beyond limits. On the one hand these limits denote the border between private life and social life or prevent us from trespassing on other human beings' living-space. On the other hand, laws also serve as a protection for human beings' innate fragility, as only this fragility and openness gives birth to new virtues and strengths.

Chastity is the clasp of protection for the individual's fragility, which at present he is usually not wise enough to use to guard against all kinds of abuse, intrusion, brutality and destruction. It may seem stupid to fence in a garden full of rare flowers; it seems as if one is fencing it off from other people's appreciation as well. When stray dogs, fleeing from famine, have trampled it, it is too late to protect it.

Each human being has such a rare and precious garden, his inner garden. Laws such as chastity serve to protect it from destruction. The fragility of the human being gives birth to many rare fruits such as tenderness, or the flowering of closeness coupled with trust and innocence, or the delicate gift of affection. All these qualities are an essential part of modern sexuality. If chastity is not there to safeguard them, these other virtues cannot pierce the hard crust and come to fruition.

In this image, the hard crust of earth can well symbolize all the destruction mankind in general and individuals have had to go through. This destruction has trampled the fruitful but fragile ground, freezing the budding of these much needed qualities that modern people crave for, but often cannot taste of yet. Brutality, inhuman behaviour, injustice, and many other odious events in the lives of people have trampled their inner garden and thus the possibility of their developing these new and essential qualities in their sexual lives, as in everything else.

Fidelity

An adulteress is stoned – is an adulterer?

Women have traditionally upheld the standard of fidelity – were they respected for doing it or belittled and laughed at behind their backs? Was it not common to think women were not having a life full of zest when they kept faithful to their husbands, minded household chores and the children? Is Penelope still our model? Who knows who she was and what she stood for? Maybe not even the Greeks speak of her very often anymore!

Fidelity (or chastity within marriage) is not a concept found very often in women's magazines, let alone men's magazines or video-strips. Where has it gone? Do marriage sermons not quietly avoid using the term?

As to chastity, this is one of the most challenging concepts to get across in this very permissive age, but Bahá'ís must make the utmost effort to uphold Bahá'í standards, no matter how difficult they may seem at first. [13]

Today's understanding of fidelity in marriage seems to imply that you remain faithful as long as you love passionately and that love is reciprocated.

What happens when one of the partners is encountering difficulties in life or is in a conflict, or when both partners have not been able to solve a mutual problem very rapidly through adequate consultation? Does fidelity then go down the drain?

Modern life has so many difficulties lying in wait for us. Human beings, it would seem, should tick as regularly and quietly as a Seamaster watch – they should be shock- and waterproof! Instead, people are becoming more and more sensitive and vulnerable. They have few principles to arm them against doubt, the fear of being abandoned and ending in loneliness.

Could it be that this art of being faithful in marriage and partnership, the fact of its having been cast away surreptitiously, and the prevalence of loneliness in the world, are linked in many ways?

Fidelity is an essential bridging quality when one of the partners is facing difficulties or when problems crop up in the relationship and have not been solved rapidly.

Indeed thy Lord loveth fidelity as found in the realm of creation, and He hath given it precedence over most of the praiseworthy qualities. ('Abdu'l-Bahá) [14]

This seems to be another of those bedrock qualities prescribed by the All-Knowing Physician, the Manifestation of God, to unlock the door to growth and thus permit relationship. It seems to be one of those rock-bottom conditions of human happiness. Today, many people, either by tradition, habit or newly-acquired "modernness" marry but don't perceive or respect any barrier to their desires outside the marriage.

Many people are quite happy to find out, when sexual activity with their partner is not fulfilling, that it is much better with a lover. They break a marriage or two, their partner does so as well — only to find out that the same rhyme is beginning again: the partner with whom they are engaged, married or involved becomes the hideous screen on which pent-up emotions are projected. Havoc is thus re-created because of this failure to work through past hurt and torment, then to lay it down and begin to live and love. They wonder, though, when things do not turn out as they would want them to do and they have not achieved lasting happiness, either at home, with their spouse, or with their "friend", why things went wrong.

It seems rather pitiful that human beings are so little conscious of their true nature as human beings and so unaware that only part of their being follows animal laws such as drive, instinct, desire, pleasure, etc.

Among the people of Bahá however, marriage must be a union of the body and of the spirit as well, for here both husband and wife are aglow with the same wine, both are enamoured of the same matchless Face, both live and move through the same spirit, both are illumined by the same glory. This connection between them is a spiritual one, hence it is a bond that will abide forever. Likewise do they enjoy strong and lasting ties in the physical world as well, for if the marriage is based both on the spirit and the body, that union is a true one, hence it will endure. If, however, the bond is physical and nothing more, it is sure to be only temporary, and must inexorably end in separation.

When, therefore, the people of Bahá undertake to marry, the union must be a true relationship, a spiritual coming together as well as a physical one, so that throughout every phase of life, and in all the worlds of God, their union will endure; for this real oneness is a gleaming out of the love of God. ('Abdu'l-Bahá)[15]

Psychologically, this is very understandable. If both partners adhere to chastity, there is a basis of equality from the outset: both have this precious gift to offer each other; neither has any desire to compare their partner with any other person; both are unique to each other. Both have full confidence in each other, as chastity and its ensuing attitude to the other sex and to erotic and sexual relationships outside of the marriage give both full freedom of interaction and full security of maintenance of the marriage relationship. There is no jealousy, no possessiveness, attitudes that hamper many a marriage from the outset. How many problems can be avoided if these terrible companions – jealousy, possessiveness and exclusiveness – are not invited into the relationship and the home!

Furthermore, it is one of the best guarantors for a happy marriage, provided, of course, that both sexes adhere strictly to it and in full consciousness of its precious aid.

Armed with the shield of chastity, partners will not hamper each other's interactions in the social sphere, but in full confidence welcome all relationships outside of the home, provided they be guided by moral standards. Friendship in its pure form is possible between men and women and between persons of the same sex; confidence and trust are part of relationships with employer and co-workers, with business partners and in all useful fields of endeavour.

Closeness and freedom

Closeness between two partners is an integral part of mature and growth-promoting sexuality.

Married for years, and parents of three children, Martin and Beatrice will be asking for separation tomorrow: they have never been able to be close to each other or to allow each other the freedom to pursue a profession in a creative way or to form personal friendships. Although they are attached to each other, they are most unhappy. Whenever they get a bit closer together, one of them flares up and they are again at a distance. When they are enjoying some freedom, jealousy draws them closer. They have never been able to solve the riddle. Resigned, they are to separate, tomorrow . . .

The quest for a balance between closeness and freedom, between intimacy and the leeway to evolve personally within legitimate bounds, is a most pressing one today. Each couple has to find their own solution. For some it comes naturally, for others it is the outcome of years of hard struggle, while others separate because they have given up.

For some the issue is particularly difficult. Those whose parents feared closeness are especially at risk. Martin's father committed suicide when Martin was a young child, while his mother lapsed into psychosis. Beatrice's father was an alcoholic and her mother had taken refuge indefinitely in abysmal depression. These two sets of parents had resorted to drastic methods of maintaining distance; like their unfortunate children, they had feared closeness and thus never achieved it, although it had been their aim.

What are the barriers to closeness? Certainly the patriarchal system, with its upholding of role-thinking and role-playing, is averse to any sort of closeness between partners in a marriage, for otherwise the rigid roles cannot be maintained.

Groping after this longed-for closeness for the first time in history, many people project such high hopes on this prized "possession" that it is impossible for them to achieve it naturally. They are afraid of being disappointed, perhaps remembering the long fights of their parents, or the cold distance they maintained in order to remain true to the roles society demanded of them.

Criticism is an enemy of closeness. The critical attitude creates a safe distance from possible hurt. Thus, when partners are both critical and vulnerable, they perforce have to maintain the distance in their relationship.

Some people are deeply afraid of being sought out in their intimacy and of their weaknesses becoming apparent. They hide from closeness.

A great gap in interests, experience or capacities can create or maintain distance instead of permitting closeness. This, however, is not always so, for many people today are learning to work on their emotional and spiritual relationship instead of harping on the differences and maintaining the gap.

What creates closeness? Simple things — the sharing of time, space, and simple interests. These foster the creation of a warm, non-judgemental atmosphere.

It is trying hard to steer clear of harping on difficulties and of criticism, and the fostering of mutual understanding.

It is consulting whenever some mishap has occurred, redeeming the distance created by anger, hurt or withdrawal.

It is explaining things to each other until the emotional distance has thawed, and warm, true emotions well up again — not leaving things askance and mid-way.

It is the courage to persist, and the hope of diminishing barriers instead of maintaining them.

Those who are dead afraid of closeness may find it helpful to begin speaking warmly to a person they are seeing for a first and last time, for instance on a long-distance plane journey: they can feel the relief of relative closeness in conversation and still maintain their defences.

Others will have to go through a lot of pain and suffering in order to thaw the artificial barriers that were drawn up at an early age to ward off too great a hurt, for instance when parents divorced, or hurt each other, or abandoned their children.

Closeness can only be maintained if paired with a fair amount of personal freedom — otherwise it deteriorates and slips into possessive love which is suffocating to the partner.

This balance of closeness and freedom has to be developed

through practice and is not easy. Also, at different stages of a marital relationship the balance may shift: lovers can never get close enough, and are overjoyed when the first child arrives. But at other times circumstances may impose a lot of distance so that the couple can cope adequately with the many tasks of their lives such as looking after businesses, professions, children, parents and properties, and fulfilling services to friends and wider circles. But if there are no moments of closeness a couple's relationship will lose its warmth and resilience, the understanding between them will be drained and they will just function like old cart-horses used to the yoke.

Tenderness

The meaning of this is that ye must show forth tenderness and love to every human being, even to your enemies, and welcome them all with unalloyed friendship, good cheer, and loving-kindness. ('Abdu'l-Bahá)[16]

Tenderness is a normal human need, and modern sexuality is viewed more and more as comprising this expression of love. If suppressed or absent in an individual and his relationship the effect can be devastating. Women, particularly, are more often expressing their absolute need of tenderness, and its absence in the relationship can be a reason of divorce for them.

Tending, sharing and caring are important daily methods in a relationship, keeping it from drying up or withering, particularly if materialism, routine, care, difficulties, tests and trials surround the lovers.

Tenderness of heart is a quality that finds expression in the tone of voice, in warmth or fondness; it is felt by the other person's heart and body. Giving expression to feelings of tenderness is a normal human and humane quality!

'Abdu'l-Bahá, who to Bahá'ís the world over is the exemplar of how to live one's life, used to express tenderness of so many beautiful shades towards all living things — animals and human beings, children and adults, men and women. 'Abdu'l-Bahá always found the adequate mode of expression: in His look, tone of voice, in His gesture, caress, embrace, or thought — and it was felt by so many thirsting and hungry people for this unique expression of love: tenderness of heart.

In some respects woman is superior to man. She is more tender-hearted, more receptive, her intuition is more intense. ('Abdu'l-Bahá)[17]

Tenderness is expressed by mothers towards their babies and small children: as they wash and dry their child tenderly, caress its soft skin, fondle it, hold it, cuddle and rock this precious child — all of this is felt as a wave of tenderness coming from this great source of goodness, the mother! Fathers also, today, may express a certain amount of fondness and tenderness when holding their child, playing with it, tendering to its needs and exchanging caresses.

This has not always been the case. I was told, for instance, that my Irish great-grandmother refused to kiss her children and that she adhered to this principle all her life! Many men, in the past, have suppressed their desire to be tender to their children, but soften up when their first grandchild is born, fondle it and play simple, tender little games with it. Or you may see a harsh, stern person who has never showed any tenderness to anyone relent and bend to purr softly to a cat and caress its shining black fur!

Watching mothers tend their children one notices that they usually have ample tenderness and fondness for their little boys, but are more wary of having to educate their little girls well and are thus stricter with them — but, it seems, little and bigger girls, and many women, have a great need for tenderness! It seems to me as though they are crying out, in their feelings, body and mind, that they need that tenderness in adulthood as they had not been blessed with it so amply in their tender years: there is a great yearning in most women I have come across.

This great, unfulfilled need for a generous share of tenderness is often suppressed until a woman reaches full maturity and has lived with her partner for years. Then it makes itself more and more heard and felt, and often the marriage partner is overwhelmed by this great need, often not well expressed. Also, most men have not learned to express tenderness, although they seem to have received an ample measure from their loving mothers, and thus are very much at a loss how to face this strange and novel need in their partner!

When sexuality becomes inhibited or comes to a full stop, and the problem seems to be with the woman, most often one of the underlying problems is the unfulfilled need of the female partner for tenderness in the relationship.

In my office I often explain to both partners that women, it seems, have a greater desire to experience tenderness in their relationships. Further, I explain, women seem to have this craving in their body to receive tenderness in loving embraces; they want to be held and protected and feel the abiding tenderness of their partner. These needs most often run counter to the urge for action, for the expression of great desire in their male partners; thus women's needs are often submerged by the more forceful urges of their partner. Then women again give in and suppress their needs, but become depressed and feel no more craving for bodily expression of the relationship. This dumbfounds their husbands!

Most human beings are willing to learn, but only in intention and in words, not in deeds, and many marriage partners have become rather deaf to their partner's wishes, particularly if they deem them extravagant or feel that they're uncomfortable to their own dear selves! When this has gone on for months, years or decades, the suppressed need for tenderness becomes a destructive force in the unconscious. It leads to revolt, depression and anxiety, and often to an irresistible desire for separation, so as not to have to live under the same roof as the tormentor: the well-meaning, but rather lazy partner.

This wish for separation and even divorce is a terrible consequence of a simple, human, modern need — tenderness!

Modern sexuality, especially in the young, is viewed as comprising tenderness; young people can become so surprisingly proficient in this art as to shock their parents (most of all rather insensitive and bumbling fathers) into the realization that their sons have gently overtaken them on this path to humaneness.

In my office, Matthew talked about his children one day — the girl being so deft at mending parental rows, the boy — a sensitive lad of 15 — being so tender towards his mother that he was able to give her all the warmth and emotional security she had never had. All of a sudden, I saw Matthew's eyes become very moist, while his voice became even squeakier than it usually was. I fell silent and waited for this sudden outbreak of emotion to ripple away, then I asked Matthew: "What touched you so much?" Still very moved, he said awkwardly, "The fact, the fact that my son can do that — be so tender!"

It is wonderful to witness, on the whole, great progress from one generation to another. Younger people are finding out about both sexes' craving for tenderness. They can also express it more freely and offer it more often as a loving gift to their partner for life.

Aid Thou Thy trusted servants to have loving and tender hearts. ('Abdu'l-Bahá)[18]

In the same way, when any souls grow to be true believers, they will attain a spiritual relationship with one another, and show forth a tenderness which is not of this world. They will, all of them, become elated from a draught of divine love, and that union of theirs, that connection, will also abide forever. Souls, that is, who will consign their own selves to oblivion, strip from themselves the defects of humankind, and unchain themselves from human bondage, will beyond any doubt be illumined with the heavenly splendours of oneness, and will all attain unto real union in the world that dieth not. ('Abdu'l-Bahá)[19]

Tenderness has cultural patterns – and barriers! The Oriental may be very tender in words, but prudish in actions – or, on the contrary, so proficient in love-making as an art that Westerners go to sleep with a copy of the *Kamasutra* under their pillow, still not knowing exactly what it means.

Tenderness can sometimes be proficiently expressed during courtship but subside like a spring river in summer heat after the marriage is consummated, never to return. This reflects the belief that it is not seemly for a man, once he has become a husband and a father, to use wooing techniques beyond the phase of courtship – after all, the male duck doesn't do it either, but struts off in male dignity to leave the female to do her duty by the eggs, and so on!

We Bahá'ís believe though that this strict role-thinking has ended and that a new era has dawned!

Although the need for tenderness in modern sexuality is great, both as a basic need of women and to enable the mellowing of the relationship, to render it humane and most of all durable (!), it should not be kept out of focus: this need must be patiently, persistently explained and exemplified, but should be kept in perspective by recognizing all the other qualities to be fostered and brought into the relationship. None of these individual needs should become so predominant as to rule out reason or endanger the relationship.

Affection

Among the manifold aspects of love, affection seems a very important one in eyes of 'Abdu'l-Bahá (He was the embodiment of affection for every creature). When Bahá'ís think of this all-pervading aspect of love, they very often think of 'Abdu'l-Bahá's unceasing affection for everyone.

If love in the form of passion is that gushing vital force which seems to contain the energy to change and recreate relationships, affection can be likened to streaming waters of a different strength: the one that sustains and perseveres. It is the warming kind of love, a source of gentle heat demanding nothing in return.

Passion seems to want an answer: do you love me — or do you reject me? Affection seems to want *to* answer. It confides in you, deposits its warming strength, and leaves it for you to use. You can absorb it, and do nothing with it for days and years, or you can bask in its sunshine. You can also let it sustain you in your endeavours. You can respond to it with that same warmth. But there seems to be no demand on you to respond, to comply or redouble in effort or with a shower of love.

Compared to a stream, gushing from the rocks in passionate appeals, affection is the ensuing phase, gliding under the cool shade of trees, harbouring minnows or trout, lapping around the stones in calm pools. Midstream it is strong and sustaining, but along the banks it adapts to the woods, the rushes, the sandbanks.

If passion is a force that conquers and abandons, affection lends a sustaining strength to two partners and to whatever grows around them.

Affection relates to qualities such as patience: it does not seem to expend its energy; on the contrary, it calls up deeper powers of life such as the patience to sustain without asking for a return.

Without being masochistic, frustrated or exasperated, the affectionate person seems to find a recompense in the act of giving rather than receiving: there seems to exist between the lovers a secret agreement that there is a return — it can be in a wink, in a nudge, or even three weeks' later when stress is over and mutual playfulness can set in again.

When a couple has moved out of the great gush of passion, out of the phase of rejection, despair, frustration and/or a dearth of love, they seem to want to naturally make their way towards affection.

Affection has a firm hold on life. It is based on mutual attraction, on a secure relationship. There is no more wrangling about who is stronger, who is dominating and who is submissive. It is a firm tie where both know that there is no more question of conquest, of sacking the citadel before abandoning it to the elements of destruction – all too often passion's negative side.

If passion can sometimes be likened to the animal drive in its human form, affection is definitely on a human plane. It is comfortable using all kinds of messages such as a look or a gesture – it is not linked to conquest!

Affection knows no abuse – it has attained those heights where abuse is neither mentioned nor thought of. Each partner fills in where the other lacks a quality or the strength to pursue the common vision. Both are weaving their thoughts and feelings, their visions and endeavours into the same cloth.

4

Some difficult relationships

RELATIONSHIP implies mutual respect and the desire to learn together and from each other. It also implies facing the various aspects of life in harmony and understanding.

Without a certain measure of respect on both sides it is not possible to maintain a positive relationship. Where there is no reciprocity, one person feels like a tyrant and vacillates between a sense of power, guilt and anger, while the other feels exploited, angry and then guilty. When a relationship is very degraded, it becomes more and more detached from reality and thus more and more destructive, ending in isolation.

An important aim of every healthy human being is to achieve harmony and understanding in an intimate relationship. In a healthy relationship it is understood that each partner acts and thinks separately in many fields, but that in some aspects of life they interact and share. In some unhappy and highly unhealthy relationships people feel imprisoned, as if they cannot break out of a closed place. This is the case with all relationships where dependency or domination are felt to be hampering growth and evolution both in the individuals and in the relationship. This, one may say, is happening more and more, and one may wonder why.

Many factors are at work, both positive and negative. On the negative side are the lack of true religion and the ensuing materialism and pursuit of pleasure, and the unwillingness to assume responsibility for building up a moral character and life-style.

On the positive side, Bahá'ís believe, is the evolution of humanity as part of God's creation. Humanity now has the choice of either following God's precepts for human nature and the age we live in, or of finding out the limits of human nature and what havoc can be wrought in individuals and in society when we do not follow these precepts.

As you point out, it is particularly difficult to follow the laws of Bahá'u'lláh in present-day society whose accepted practice is so at variance with the standards of the Faith. However, there are certain laws that are so fundamental to the healthy functioning of human society that they must be upheld whatever the circumstances. Realizing the degree of human frailty, Bahá'u'lláh has provided that other laws are to be applied only gradually, but these too, once they are applied, must be followed, or else society will not be reformed but will sink into an ever worsening condition. It is the challenging task of the Bahá'ís to obey the law of God in their own lives, and gradually to win the rest of mankind to its acceptance.[1]

It certainly seems as if we were nearing rock-bottom in this process of sinking low morally, both in individual lives and in that of society! In some relationships, one partner or the other has a deficiency in his personality that severely hampers the relationship; the partners are unable to cooperate in the gradual healing of the deficiency. Jealousy, for instance, or envy, are crippling deficiencies and influence intimate relationships severely.

Jealousy

Sheila has been married for years and has teenage children. Recently she became depressed and lost her appetite, resulting in loss of weight. In therapy it appeared that she had been trying for years to cope with rising jealousy, but had given up hope of ever overcoming this crippling handicap. As a child and an adolescent she had been the witness of her parents' almost daily scenes of jealousy and violence with the threat of suicide and murder, and thus she had become adamant in her resolve never to become jealous as her mother had been. Over the years, as her jealousy rose, she was struck with fear of coming to resemble her mother more and more. Her husband knew about her jealousy, but couldn't understand his wife's fear of becoming like her mother and continued commenting favourably on women's looks and behaviour in the street. Sheila felt she was incapable of coping with the situation any longer; she sought therapy and brought her husband with her. Both of them had to learn to face the problem both of Sheila and their relationship, and to learn to bridge the gap that had been created through the fact that they had not been coping with this very serious issue in their marriage.

Jealousy consumeth the body and anger doth burn the liver; avoid these two as you would a lion. (Bahá'u'lláh)[2]

How true is this profound saying from the Bahá'í Writings, and how often a physician will find this confirmed when treating people!

Today all people are immersed in the world of nature. That is why thou dost see jealousy, greed, the struggle for survival . . . which all emanate from the world of nature. Few are those who have been freed from this darkness, who have ascended from the world of nature to the world of man . . . ('Abdu'l-Bahá)[3]

Envy

Envy is another severe handicap in a relationship. When envy, whether of possessions, qualities or achievements, is part of the relationship, all good aspects linking the two are slowly sapped. A void ensues, which then is filled with emotions such as anger, hate, and the desire to destroy the happiness and achievements of the other person.

Envy is part of the lower or animal nature of man. Any educator of a child, whether the parents or the teachers, can readily perceive this ingredient in the child's imperfect coping with relationships and with reality. The educator will then have to patiently help remedy this deficiency in the child and wean it away from this most unfortunate ingredient of so many sibling relationships. Both envy and jealousy are learned in the family; they are to be found most often in highly immature families, where siblings have the feeling of not receiving due attention from parents and then act out their unhappiness towards their brothers or sisters – or sometimes towards the parents themselves!

"Know, verily, the heart wherein the least remnant of envy yet lingers, shall never attain My everlasting dominion, nor inhale the sweet savours of holiness breathing from My kingdom of sanctity," Bahá'u'lláh says in the *Hidden Words*.[4]

Having to be right

The fact that we imagine ourselves to be right and everybody else wrong is the greatest of all obstacles in the path towards unity, and unity is necessary if we would reach truth, for truth is one. ('Abdu'l-Bahá)[5]

"Thomas is going right ahead with this thing. Of course he doesn't know how to do it. I told him what to do but he just can't listen. Now everything is going wrong. I told him: you see, you should have listened to me!" Thus the highly opinionated wife of a businessman whose affairs were quickly moving towards bankruptcy. Both husband and wife were sure that they were doing the right thing, and spent hours and days telling each other off. In the meanwhile, their affairs and also their relationship were moving towards the brink of calamity.

But both of them liked the excitement of brinkmanship, and so preferred to go on in the same vein.

René's wife is a little, bird-like creature from an exotic country who prefers dreaming to confronting bold, hefty René. Being a teacher, René loves to educate people, first of all his little wife. He tells her hour by hour how and when to do things. His wife says nothing, but she becomes depressive and drinks too much. René still goes on telling her.

In both these couples each person liked to be right – one showed it verbally, the other by not complying with the injunctions of the spouse. All were adamant in their desire to follow their own course of ingrained beliefs. None would depart from the decided track; to give in would be tantamount to giving up one's personality.

The sensitive and the insensitive

"You look fine, my dear," says the husband confidently to his hard-working, proud and sensitive wife. Inside, the wife doesn't feel at all understood by her well-meaning husband, but how can she tell him she's exhausted and on the verge of depression ? She clams up, bites her lip, and goes on until she collapses and has to go to hospital for two months. The husband doesn't understand what has happened and is very worried, as he adores his wife and needs her desperately to function well in everyday life.

Sensitivity to others is becoming a very necessary quality. It allows a person to understand situations when communication is non-verbal, through the atmosphere among people, in a room, in the family or at work, through gestures and the tone of voice. Verbal communication does not always touch on important inner meanings and beliefs. In today's society we often see people who are over-sensitive reacting to every hurt, while others bungle about happily with heavy boots not realizing they're treading on fragile ground and other people's delicate feelings.

So it seems that some will have to learn not to react, but to protect their vulnerability in a competent way. Others will have to acquire sensitivity. Both these developments usually come about only through suffering.

How can a sensitive partner help an insensitive companion on the road to sensitivity ? Could it be that the sensitive one will have to allow the partner to go through some heartbreak and thus realize certain facts of life ?

The spendthrift and the tightfisted

In this configuration, economy may be a quality both partners appreciate, but their interpretation of it may vary considerably and thus make them suffer!

Robert and Barbara each came from a very modest background where their parents had been forced to practise strict economy. Robert sensed how much his mother had suffered from this constant constraint in her life, and felt that his father would have wanted to have a huge fling once in a while if he had more money, perhaps throwing a party in an expensive restaurant for all his friends. So once Robert was a teenager, his parents' hidden frustrations and desires began to be lived out in Robert's own behaviour. He became an expert spendthrift: he loved to dine out in exclusive restaurants and take taxis everywhere — and he was very generous towards his friends; he always invited them all home for an extended "night-cap" before they hilariously tottered off to bed. Barbara had learned the opposite lesson: she became very careful with money and thus always had the feeling of still having a little leeway in case things became even tighter.

When their relationship began they felt they complemented one another, and this was part of their mutual attraction. Later, they felt conflict growing between them, but fearing an open struggle they became polite but distant. In time, Barbara couldn't face Robert's flings anymore, and in spite of real attachment she left him. Robert felt totally abandoned and went to seed within a few years.

The orderly and the "artistic"

Florence had an artistic vein and her studio had lots of atmosphere. That was what attracted Barney, who came from a very orderly but rather staid family. Barney's little apartment was spick and span, everything in its right place, stuck away in drawers and cupboards. It felt like an office or a hotel but not like a home. He moved in with Florence, but soon found that it was very difficult for him to see the icebox cluttered and unwashed, or to have to put away more and more things when Florence wasn't feeling well, rather like a strict mum.

They liked each other's companionship and decided to consult together to find a way out of this dilemma. Florence explained to Barney that she felt cramped by his extreme orderliness, but because she admired it she fought her tendency to be easy-going and happy-go-lucky in household affairs. Barney soothed Florence by telling her how much he appreciated the atmosphere she created and her sense of colour and hospitality, but that he sometimes felt like the garbage-man when the disorder and sloppiness reached his threshold of pain and he had to clean up for two.

They decided to give each other six more months, to consult every week for at least an hour on how to make things better for both of them. If things became better, they would find a larger apartment and agree on certain rules, leaving each of them free in certain aspects of life but trying to adhere to common standards where they shared space and time.

It was around this time that they came to know a few Bahá'ís and learned how to consult and especially about the importance of putting decisions into action. Things became better. It seemed stupid not to show how much they were committed to each other and to family and friends. They got married.

The hyper-sexual and the prudish

"My wife is a prude — and I really am into sex!" Such a pair is encountered rather often. Owing to cultural patterns and the social climate, it is frequently the men who are "into" sex and the women who are "prudes", especially in older generations. Things are changing, though, and many a young woman may be proud of being more interested in sex than her boyfriend is.

Such a mismatch can lead to much heartbreak, as both will use heavy weapons to defend their cause. "Sex is an instinct we have in common with animals, it's part of our bodily functions and needs, and we should not suppress it." Those who are believers in a beneficent Creator will rightly say sex is part of God's creation. Sex is normal, natural, and relaxing — "Look at her, she's cramped and hurting all over her back: that's surely because she's suppressed her rightful instincts! And then, instead of sleeping deeply, she tosses and turns!"

The counterpart will argue: "No delicacy, no tenderness, as long as he can sink his jaws into a big piece of meat — just IT, nothing else! Just the raw beast, nothing humane, no refinement, nothing cultural, no communication except for raw sex! And as soon as it's done with, off he goes, deep asleep and snoring, whilst I'm all knots inside, all cramped, and totally frustrated at not having been respected as a human being! Then I toss and turn until morning. And after all this he wonders why I don't want anything to do with it, except to keep him quiet! When I'm at my wits' end I wish he'd get a mistress — but then, I'm terribly afraid and jealous, you know. I really couldn't bear it. I'd rather die!"

The oppositional character

One of the stages of child development is the oppositional phase. A child will take pleasure in asserting his own will, particularly if it is contrary to his mother's wishes and instructions. This, psychologists confirm, is an important phase for the child so that it can develop consciousness of self as opposed to other people.

For the child subsequently to move out of this phase, warm understanding and support on the part of the mother are needed. The child needs to be assured that the parent is happy to see the child develop, but will protect it from danger and bad behaviour. If the mother is too insecure herself to let the child go, it remains stuck in this phase, particularly if it takes pleasure in the "naughty" game – and wins. People who have stuck in this phase have not developed their own self and their own values, but tend to react to other people's assertions and actions. Their way of trying to be assertive is to oppose the other person, even to their own detriment. They do not seem to have any other way of taking action.

Lucy's husband is a good-natured man who gets on well with his colleagues at work, including the women he supervises as a foreman. Lucy is incapable of seeing the good side of Mark, but gets so wound up in opposition to him that Mark gets sick of her and turns to a mistress, although he really likes his family and his wife. It takes Lucy a long time to disentangle herself from this early way of reacting to people near to her.

The partner as garbage bin

One of the main causes of sexual dysfunction is the common habit of treating one's partner as one's daily garbage bin, while remaining all the while unconscious of the situation and its unhappy consequences.

For instance, a man has to cope with many frustrations at his work place. There he cannot get rid of them, but as soon as he gets home he treats his wife poorly, complains about her not having done things properly, not being attentive enough and most of all not being a good and sensitive lover to him.

A woman has had an extremely trying day with her three young children, so as soon as her husband comes home she whines and complains about how unhappy she is to have to stay at home to look after his children.

Both these people have treated their partner as a garbage bin. They are not at all conscious of what they're doing: they have thrown a lot of garbage into the bin but have not gone to empty it in the back yard – the garbage bin is being emptied in bed, i.e. towards the lover.

Sado-masochistic relationships

It is very difficult to describe these relationships – probably the most exquisitely painful to be imagined. And they are terribly characteristic of our modern times.

Two persons are locked into each other's flesh with jaws clenched. To tear away would be tantamount to death. A part of each person's personality seems irrevocably imprisoned in the other person.

An outsider often very much wants to help a person locked into such a terrible relationship. The person certainly is a victim – he even seems to be the only victim! But should the outsider become enmeshed as well, he becomes a party to the conflict and goes on taking sides, lending weight to one side and thus provoking the other side to look for more help. The conflict becomes bigger and bigger. Thus, these pathetic relationships often end up with everyone taking sides: family, neighbours, friends, teachers, doctors, social workers, lawyers, local government officials – and the conflict is still unsolved!

Its dimensions have grown, it towers above the suffering, the helpers, the therapists — unsolved!

How do these relationships come about?
There is a great dependency in the way that neither of the parties feels complete enough to be a person. Thus, one person can be acting as the brain of the other, or the feelings of his spouse. The other, though, is the responsible person and organizes the whole, has the strength to cope. One deals with outsiders, the other with the family. As long as things go smoothly, such a kind of dependency does not become degraded. But should one of the partners become vulnerable and not be able to defend himself or herself, neither in word nor deed, the basis for hurt and ensuing revenge is laid. A new game begins: the game of torment and revenge, of hurt and slashing back in a different way.

Both become tormentors, both are hurt, both take revenge. Both are victims. How do you move out of such torment? You can become numb, and let go. You can begin to take in the situation and to act in a positive sense, beginning to change your own attitudes and reactions. This usually takes years before it is felt in the relationship. Also, it doesn't happen without help — and it is difficult to find good and wise help!

Why are women such perfect victims?
This is difficult to understand if not seen in a historical perspective. Women, as you know, were counted among the cattle in many countries not so long ago. In our own so-called advanced civilization, it was only in 1835 that the Pope decreed that women have a soul! I believe the unconscious of most men has not awoken to the fact that women do have a soul and are responsible beings.

If you'd like an image, it is like a hunter stabbing an animal. While the animal is in agony, panting for life, the hunter triumphantly puts his foot on it and boasts, "These poor beasts have no courage to stand up for themselves!"

Why are men not conscious of this fact?
Because it would be too uncomfortable – it would necessitate a change of attitude and of life-style. For any human being beyond puberty this is a source of anguish and anxiety, linked with feelings of helplessness, frustration and depression. It is not easy to change – much easier to remain unconscious and thus protected from realizing, painfully, how much men are contributing to this situation.

Why are men perfect victims?
They are very vulnerable to public opinion, in other words, to the image they project onto others, be it family members (including their own children), neighbours, employees or employers, or anyone they want to impress. Women know this, either consciously or unconsciously – and they are apt to use deflating words, either in backbiting or in calumny, to lash back at the oppressor. The man then truly *will* become an oppressor! His pride, linked as it is to his image, is hurt to the quick.

Women also use a kind of moral superiority to judge a man – without a word, or with small, cutting comments. "You're lazy, you never help"; "You don't care enough for your children to stay home and play with them"; "Sport, or politics, or your mates down at the pub, or your new stereo/ video recorder/football boots/Porsche are more important to you than your relationship with your wife or your son", etc.

It is very difficult to ward off such judgements. They hurt. They contain an uncomfortable appeal for change.

Why do women continue to use these deadly weapons, weapons that are condemned both by ethics and religion?
They too would have to change. And changing is difficult. They would have to work on themselves, learn to have goals

and priorities in life apart from the one of serving and pleasing family members. They would have to learn to speak for themselves and defend themselves.

Some other pathological relationships

Some relationships are so lacunary that one can only call them one-sided or tentative, as there is no commitment of any kind. One of these is the "bed-and-breakfast" type, a relationship on such a low and basic level as to be subhuman. Despite this, it's quite prevalent today, when so many people are profoundly disappointed, both by their parents' failure to establish a good and durable relationship and by having themselves undergone shipwreck, often more than once.

Another type is the one of the cat, creeping in through the half-open barn door at dusk and slipping out again next day.

Ruth suffered disastrously from her parents' relationship, and deep inside something guarded her against ever having the same experience. She has three darling children. The father is a foreigner who turns up now and then in Ruth's welcoming but simple apartment, where he is almost like a fourth child. When he hasn't shown his face for a certain length of time Ruth says equitably, "I guess he's committed some larceny again and landed in prison for the winter." Neither Ruth nor her man have any basic trust in the opposite sex. Ruth had a loving relationship with her quiet and sheepish father who died early, thus evading the "general's" sempiternal rule. Her partner had a "good mama" who never told him off and never guided him, but always fed and clothed him whenever he was around.

Another of these relationships is based on the well-named "Casanova complex". In this game the man is ever out to besiege the fortress, but when it yields he sacks it and leaves for another one. The woman (the fortress) is at first stand-offish, then shy or defiant. Finally, under the pressure of much tenderness and attention, she yields. When she is bemoaning her plight — not much later — she says: "I knew he was no good, like my brother. But he was so kind, so tender, so full of little attentions . . . he was so sweet — but all of a sudden, he didn't show up again. And I was so much in love with him, in the end!"

* * *

What, the reader may wonder, do unhappy or complicated, frustrating relationships have to do with sexuality?

It seems to be a more and more prevalent pattern that men and women on the one hand make great efforts to form harmonious relationships and thus open up to a warm and natural sexual relationship, but that on the other hand they hold in the many grievances and hurts sustained in difficult relationships such as those described above. "Our body does not lie", is a psychological axiom. Thus, many people express their psychological hurts in a marred sex life, or tell each other off before, during and after sexual activity because they feel vulnerable then and have temporarily lost restraint. Of course, the quality of sex life is deeply affected by an unhappy relationship. Also, sex itself may become the weapon in a difficult relationship where there is no respect, as in the case of the "hipped" and the "prudish".

In the end, people will have to make up their minds whether they are willing to work on their characters and also learn to consult. These are two of the best remedies to mend and even heal such unhappy relationships. Such people must arm themselves with patience and hope: the process can be a long but a rewarding one.

There is a difference between character and faith; it is often very hard to accept this fact and put up with it, but the fact remains that a person may believe in and love the Cause — even to being ready to die for it – and yet not have a good personal character, or possess traits at variance with the teachings. We should try to change, to let the Power of God help recreate us and make us true Bahá'ís in deed as well as in belief. But sometimes the process is slow, sometimes it never happens because the individual does not try hard enough. But these things cause us suffering and are a test to us . . . (Shoghi Effendi)[6]

5

Immature and degrading relationships

Three wheels . . .

"I've been living with my husband for fifteen years now, but three years ago I fell in love with my neighbour, and he has become my lover. I want to leave my husband, but I don't want to live with my friend: he's married too and he doesn't want to break up his marriage. Besides, he's a tyrant, like my father, and I don't want to live with a tyrant. But my husband never replies to my questions, never answers, never takes a stand, never decides, and I just don't love him! But the children . . . what should I do?"

"With my wife I share my everyday life, my children, the household, I help her out with the shop — but she doesn't know I have all kinds of romances outside of the marriage. Women are so mysterious, so attractive. I'm finding out about them . . ."

What makes people want to go on with a trusted spouse and have a secret lover at the same time? It is, of course, part of our "free", hedonistic and individualistic society: if it pleases me, and I like it, what keeps me from seeking what I crave ? We only live once, and we have to enjoy life as much as we can, we

66

never know what will be coming tomorrow! After all, my wife (my husband) doesn't know about it and we go on as if everything were fine – and I am fond of my partner, no doubt about it! I could never leave my life-companion, nor the children. I'm really very attached to my family and my home . . .

People who entertain such an arrangement for some time keep up the facade. They go along with traditional values, they don't want to disturb age-long patterns in their family, or in the neighbourhood or village they live in. They adapt too well, on the one hand, to what is expected of them, without believing in the values that formerly animated this traditional pattern: faithfulness, truthfulness, honesty. They believe the traditional patterns provide comfort and stability and don't "mess up" things. Adapting well to the pattern handed down to them means they accept the authoritarian tradition, but in name only, while revolt undermines their inner being. They have little civil courage, as it were – they dare not go against the prevailing order. Also, they are afraid of the ostracism that might ensue, the loneliness and discomfort.

Torn between comfort, the warmth of family life and the adventure and zest of pleasures outside the marriage, these people have developed few basic values apart from the materialistic ones of a need for comfort, well-being and stability without too many of the risks inherent to life and its swift movement. A certain shallowness has crept into their daily life, so much geared to the physical necessities. Or course, the more the inner being gets lost in the confusion of materialism, the more people try to grasp something – anything – to fill the gap.

This mortal life is sure to perish; its pleasures are bound to fade away and ere long ye shall return unto God, distressed with pangs of remorse, for presently ye shall be roused from your slumber, and ye shall soon find yourselves in the presence of God and will be asked of your doings. (The Báb)[1]

Following the shallowness comes a confusion about values and goals in life. The traditional values adhered to outwardly are not really convincing enough. The great changes in life and society have not found roots in corresponding concepts, ethics and beliefs to make overall change possible in the personality too.

Also, much of the routine, of the aversion to change, is projected onto the spouse who seems traditional, stable and comfortably embedded in a narrow world of business or of home and children.

One nice young couple had been extremely unhappy with their respective childhoods and upbringings and had looked for new ways. Very lonely in this search, they felt basically insecure. The only way to retain some semblance of security was for the man to pursue a traditional career, and thus gain some admiration from his colleagues and his boss, and for the wife to become a perfect housewife, searching out the best soaps and detergents and the cheapest nappies, and managing the children so that they would always be orderly and clean. Inside these two were insecure, but this facade of normality – "we're normal people, like everyone" – was necessary to their insecure selves.

Whenever challenged, the wife would flare up and pretend she would love to change and become more adventurous, but that her husband was so terribly chained to the notion of his career as to make change impossible to her. And when the selfsame question was put to the husband he was very open to new idea – he was generally open to ideas – but his wife was so fastidious and compulsively clean that he just couldn't change.

In the end people become apathetic and discouraged, having lost their zest for life. They cling to routine and the semblance of things, but become alienated from their true selves and also from life which is changing so rapidly!

Psychologically, then, people want to find a new zest to life, some pep — and the best and fastest way seems to be to give in to that strong craving for sexual stimulation and pleasure with a person other than the partner: the man who has a good house-body at home will be looking for a flashy, dynamic or sexy creature, the woman who has a good father to her children but a rather lazy and egocentric lover will be out for a seducer and a flatterer of her rapidly waning beauty.

"How come you went along for fifteen years with a marriage where, as you say, there was no love, and you didn't want to change anything?" I asked the woman who was so torn between her husband and her lover.

"I don't know — I just went along with it. It suited me and him, I guess. But now it doesn't suit me any more. I'd like to change things, but he doesn't want to."

"Have you spoken to him about your feelings?"

"I've tried — but it's not easy, he just doesn't answer, he grumbles, or smiles, and goes upstairs and has a swig. I just can't take it any more."

This woman is now going through a painful therapy working through dramatic childhood experiences of incest. In fact, her marriage came about in the first place so as not to incommodate her father whose employee her husband was. Trying to change the marriage meant working through some of the relationship with the father, who was an autocrat. This woman had a habit of compulsive adaptation to other people's needs. She kept up an image of being good, responsible and reliable, at the cost of her own needs of health and happiness. She had not learned legitimate ways of speaking up for her values (she is sober, good-hearted and family-minded). Her bad self-image made it easy for her father's (and husband's) tyrannical wishes to get the better of her. Unfortunately, her son too was developing tyrannical habits.

The modern phenomenon of an extramarital relationship is a dead-end to growth and the maturing of relationship — both in the marriage and in the extramarital affair. It is satisfactory for a time and on certain levels, but is doomed to come to a standstill. This is divine decree!

How to emerge from this predicament? By taking a decision. One possibility is to quit the mistress/lover (which is usually the right decision) and to begin to investigate the state of affairs at home, with the determination to solve long-standing problems. Separation may be an answer, if the situation at home is unbearable and the partner in spite of an honest appeal refuses to cooperate. Separation in this instance is a means to solving the problem and not necessarily the first step inevitably leading to divorce.

Often the determination to solve problems opens doors to deeper understanding, touches the hardened heart of a partner or makes him or her realize the value of the relationship and to wish to revert from destructive habits. This is then the beginning of an opening into a new phase of the relationship.

In very few instances an extramarital affair is the consequence of a dead relationship at home. Then the person should go through the process of separation and divorce before envisaging another relationship; otherwise the same flaws, difficulties and conflicts will be carried into the new relationship. So in any case the person will have to begin clearing up long-standing personal problems and grow, so as to be able to form a new, healthier relationship.

Incestuous relationships and sexual abuse

Some years ago an American source quoted statistics to the effect that one in four women in the United States has been sexually abused before adulthood.

This is a terrible statement! It means that the most frank and open society in the world has admitted that one quarter of its entire female population has undergone sexual abuse. How big is the rest of the iceberg?

These shocking figures prompted more research into a

subject which had been taboo. World Health Organization studies suggest that as many as one-third of the adult female population and one-fifth of the adult male population have experienced some form of sexual abuse in childhood and very similar rates have been found in the 14 countries surveyed. A recent Canadian survey has revealed that one in two women has been subjected to sexual abuse − 80% in the form of incest! World statistics now speak of 170 million children being sexually abused each year, 90% of them female children.

Incest and abuse are part of the dark side of human sexuality. They lurk in a surprisingly high percentage of relationships and families, of all countries and social classes. This is a particular challenge of our times, for it is only in the last few years that much information has come to the surface. The sense of taboo, and also the interests vested in organized crime of this kind − such as "sex tourism" marketed to Westerners in the form of package tours to developing countries where children are forced to work as prostitutes for this specialized tourist trade − has made it well-nigh impossible for victims to find a hearing ear and a non-judgemental attitude on the part of parents, social workers, the police and the judiciary. This has been particularly true of incest, which accounts for a great percentage of abuse in children and adolescents.

Incest and past abuse is devastating to healthy sexuality and cripples relationships. Can it be imagined that abuse, and most of all incest at an early age where the abuser is a parent or a sibling, can produce human beings who are healthy and not maimed? Can one believe that the abusers are happy, balanced and responsible human beings, in relation to their partners as well as generally?

When, in 1991, I attended the 5th UN Congress on incest, I was profoundly moved not only by such statistics, but also by the sincere efforts on the part of many judges, therapists, volunteers and self-help groups to assist the victims and perpetrators of sexual abuse. It is becoming evident that our societies harbour not only cancerous individuals, institutions and agents, but also many dedicated and sincere individuals, institutions and agents who are making open, patient and courageous efforts to straighten out these situations.

The facts make it clear that in many parts of the world, in many societies generally and for the vast majority of individuals, sexuality is not yet the expression of love and affection, and the desire to communicate these to a life partner. But when these are absent, sexuality has more to do with the expression of absolute power of the strong over the weak or even the helpless. It becomes the expression of lust, or egotism, or even the impulse to destroy, as is the case in serial killings, for example. It can also be a lucrative way of filling one's pockets, as in pornography or films of abused children (who are often then killed).

The Greeks created the myth of Pandora, whom the Gods had forbidden to open a certain box. She, however, could not resist, and when she opened the lid, unnamed forbidding ills poured out. Could one of these ills coming out of Pandora's box be the consciousness of sexual abuse that has taken place in women's early lives and the ensuing consequences?

Could one of the ensuing consequences of the abuse of women of all ages, but most of all in their tender years, be their passivity resulting from untold fears of the power wielded by men, and of their cruelty?

Could another of the consequences be the still prevalent frigidity and basic unresponsiveness of women? Are they still in their inmost feelings battling with the conviction that as soon as they relent and give in to their natural need for touch or even passion they will be overpowered and abused – again?

Could the more fearful nature of women, those "unrealistic" fears women have, so often brushed aside as part of their "hysterical" nature, stem from a basic reality pertaining to the feminine condition? That woman's identity as female gives her the feeling that she has to guard, from her tender years, against men's hungry look, always wanting, always craving women, exploiting their guileless and childish ways and dumb goodness?

Could another of the consequences of Pandora's open box be that women feel so ashamed of their helpless condition, and so guilty of being tempting to men's lust, that they clam up as women, becoming hardened and competent, but hiding their feminine nature from men's perception, while suffering from their own lack of femininity in general life?

Further, could it be that this is one reason why men have not learned to treat women as people? Could they thus feel deprived of some stimulus essential to investigate a reality closed to their usually investigative, open and frank nature?

Again, could this be one reason why men, deprived of the refining tastes and influence of women's more tender and loving nature (because women clam up and close up, showing indifference, wariness and even hardness to men in spite of a seething desire to relate), remain uncouth, bumbling, technical and rational instead of integrating certain feminine traits and influences into their lives – is this why they find it so difficult to learn from women?

And, could it be that men thus have been deprived of integrating more feminine strategies of conflict resolution and peace-making into the world's system?

. . . when perfect equality shall be established between men and women, peace may be realized for the simple reason that womankind in general will never favour warfare. ('Abdu'l-Bahá)[2]

Incest and sexual abuse are not always obvious. Damage will be caused by incestuous or abusive relations even where incest is not actually carried out in practice. The examples that follow illustrate this, and are necessarily explicit. They are not intended to offend, but I recognize that some readers may find them difficult. Yet since stories like these are happening to more and more people, and being revealed more frequently, they will have to be understood before solutions can be found on any large scale.

* * *

Cathleen lies idly in the bath-tub waiting for the water to cool before she gets on with the job of scrubbing herself, so as to postpone as long as possible the moment when she will have to get out and leave this tender element she needs so much and doesn't seem to find elsewhere in life. Her father comes into the bathroom and looks her up and down in a way that touches her deeply, although she dare not think what it means. Her father even ventures to offer his services to wash her back. She rather unwillingly accepts, offers no resistance, but her inner being cringes when he washes not only her back but her sexual organs, demonstrating his own suppressed needs. The young girl dare not react: her father has beaten her all her life and often has violent outbursts of uncontrollable temper, but from then on she is careful to lock the bathroom door when having a bath or shower. She senses that the locked door is a fragile attempt to fend off something potent and uncontrollable. Consciously she never dares to think about all this – the consequences would be so great and terrible that they would rock her life and that of her family – a family so normal to outward seeming, but so fragile in reality.

Deep down she remembers the many times in her childhood when her father, usually at the bidding of her mother, had beaten her soundly for some offence – she seemed to have continuously driven the poor man into a rage over her unruliness. Somehow, there was something very intense, ominous, a restrained passion, in these regular beatings – something the little girl seemed to fear, challenge and also enjoy, for she held out in these thrashings and retreated into herself. Much later it flashed into her mind that deep inside she was screaming out to her father, "I won't give in – you can beat me to death, I'm not yielding an inch."

Later on she understood how deadly the relationship of her parents had been. She understood this when their hidden hostility to each other broke out into vituperation, baring their deep-rooted hate in an unending and entrenched war that would end only with death. She then understood that it was not the "fault" of her father – nor of her unhappy, trapped mother.

Her mother had wanted to become a pianist, but instead, when she unexpectedly sensed the faint stirrings of this first baby girl in her womb, she gave up responsibility for her own life and yielded to social pressure, her parents' insistence and her own bad conscience – and married the father of the child. Instead of a pianist, she became a housewife educating three little girls. She never was able to relate to her first child, although she did her best, materially and also on principle.

The mother in her torpor was usually not very aware of her husband's sexual needs, or only enough to find unending excuses for not giving in too often to his potent and probably normal demands: she was too tired, she had a headache or a backache, she had her period, etc. Her husband would not bully her – he was an affable person, respected by many people who saw him as a principled and competent businessman.

Sometimes, coming out of her torpor and out of a sense of duty to her first child – who was exceptionally attractive with her luscious red hair, thoughtful green eyes and lithe body – she would say peremptorily : "Cathleen, you must go and put on a top over your bra – although it's hot, it's not a good thing to eat with only a bra on." Cathleen, whose young body was avidly absorbing the sun, would look at her mother, refrain from enquiring, and dutifully go and put on a top so she could go on eating her crisp salads. But it didn't make sense to Cathleen . . . what was it her mother was trying to say? What was the nameless?

During this time two things developed in the family's habits: the father became enthusiastic about sauna baths and invited his little girls to join him at the public sauna. But mother developed an aversion to sauna! Cathleen, who enjoyed the sensations of heat and cold on her body (she was a sensual little girl), was nonetheless riveted with fear because her father, during those leisurely afternoons, could not take his eyes off her lithe cat-like body steaming in the heat, lying so naturally and still so warily on the dry benches. She never was able to wash off the unhealthy feeling of those tortured eyes on her young body. Later on, during therapy, she realized how much this had awakened her to give in early to sensuality and that this rising passion of her father for her body had impelled her to leave home at sixteen years old. She fled to a friend's house and broke off her education — but the friend's husband became her first lover! Fleeing from home, however, permitted her to save some healthy feelings and parts of her.

Cathleen had developed no efficient protection against men's lust, for she sensed her own tremendous need for love and tenderness, for affection, interest and admiration. Men could partly, and furtively, satisfy this terrible need. Cathleen had never felt this tender love on the part of her mother, who had not been available for her.

The other thing that developed was a recurrent need for Cathleen and her father to burst into violent rows once Cathleen became a teenager. They cursed and reviled each other. These rows left the father (who really was a *pater familias*) with a lot of hurt pride. He hurled threats at her while Cathleen sat weeping and sobbing in a corner. Still, Cathleen felt an indescribable triumph and satisfaction welling up in her after the terrible hurt in her heart had subsided: she had not given in! And she had vindicated her battered mother, so passive, so abused as a woman and an artist.

Cathleen realized later on that this periodic need for rows, and formerly for beatings, was a crude way of releasing pent-up sexual need in her childish, irresponsible father, and that he was only dimly aware of the terrible damage he was inflicting on his child.

*   *   *

Margaret was a sensitive, deeply reflective child of great gifts, but she was very much left to herself by absorbed and idealistic but rather unrealistic parents. Her parents were often away in the evening and her mother used to arrange for a benevolent friend, a single man in his early fifties, to come and baby-sit the children. Margaret's wide eyes became even wider and her soft brown eyes even darker when this seemingly benevolent "uncle" fondled her genitals while looking at television with her on his knees once the little boy had been put to bed. Margaret then tried to communicate this highly upsetting incident to her mother, but the mother was too much absorbed by other things and clung to her idealistic picture of this man to whom she entrusted her children. So, Margaret's genitals were fondled a few times more until Margaret understood that she would have to deal herself with this "nice uncle's" queer behaviour when her parents and her little brother were not present: she would go to bed at the same time as her brother went, pretending to be sleepy. The "nice uncle" was nice enough not to insist.

A little later on Margaret, very timid but friendly, had developed a careful relationship with the crowd of children in her neighbourhood. One evening, just as night was falling, the girls were playing hopscotch on the deserted street when they heard the voice of a man in the thick hedge of a huge house looming nearby. Margaret barely knew the owners of the house. The man was retired, having been an officer in the army. His coaxing voice now invited the little girls to come into the garden to play. Shocked into silence but instantly aware of some unseen, hideous danger, the crowd of formerly chattering girls flew away from the gloomy street and the garden with its thick hedges, into the lighted hall of one of the families where they chattered with fear, excitement and wonderment, incessantly telling the astonished mother something she could not quite grasp.

When Margaret went to school, she was a wide-eyed, timid but eager and serious pupil, a favourite of her teacher, who began singling her out when she was 9 or 10, asking her to stay over and help him sort things after class. As time went on, he would invite the little girl to his side when he was correcting the never-ending tests, and begin to fondle her little body, so warm and cuddly next to his lonely and aching one (he had four little brats at home, and a fat wife overtaxed in her strength).

Then he kissed her little face and smothered her lips with wet kisses (she didn't like those at all). Margaret was torn inside between her terrible need for affection (there was not much at home although her parents were benevolent and well-meaning) and her sense of danger and of being engulfed into something terrible, with no end to pain and suffering. She felt this poor teacher's loneliness, yes, and she wanted to help him – but in the end, one day, she did open up to her mother and rather frankly answered mother's questions. The mother then closed the subject and didn't bother the little girl any more: awakened to her responsibility, and being basically an intelligent woman, she dealt with the predicament in an efficient way. Some time later, the teacher looked sad and distant as he took leave of Margaret, telling her that he and his family were to leave for a rural area. Margaret was relieved but sad. Something went on aching but also yearning in her. Margaret had become a lonely child. How could she face these unspeakable things nestled so uncomfortably in her bosom, and how could she deal with them when there was no possibility of disclosing them without shame and guilt? She clammed up. She felt unending pain.

* * *

The stories of Cathleen and Margaret are stories of little girls' uncomfortable secret sores. What became of these girls as they grew up? One, Cathleen, sabotaged her education and had affair after affair with men, clinging to them and still not feeling sexually aroused or fulfilled. She gave up hope of ever receiving what she craved. The other girl, Margaret, felt for the men who abused her, felt guilt and shame and closed up on her pain. She became lonesome, inside and out. Approaching men was difficult for her, all the more so as she was highly intelligent and often more intelligent than the men.

What are some of the salient features of these little girls' stories where abuse did not end in incest, but where the relationship to the father was of an incestuous nature in the case of Cathleen and where sexual abuse had been carried out by people in a position of trust in the case of Margaret?

Cathleen's father was immature, with rigid principles that still restrained him from acting out his impetuous sexual needs in an overtly sexual activity with his little daughter. The need was deviated and expressed through beatings or violent rows or looks. Margaret, on the other hand, turned away from her rather absent father and looked for fatherly love and affection in other men's arms.

Cathleen's mother, in turn, was a capable woman with ambition to do something of her own in life, but was not strong enough to stand up for her own rights and defend them. Thus she succumbed to old authoritarian or puritanical principles. She gave in to the traditional scheme of a woman's life, without being able to lead the process of emancipation of her capacities and goals into useful fields. Such women usually disappear into depression, or flee their duties at home through daydreaming, or turn their back resolutely on their children's emotional needs, becoming blind most of all to what is happening to their daughters. Such women are absent, in that they are not able to protect their daughters from the needs of a father who is famished for sexual activity — and the woman cringes from this sexual activity and unconsciously leaves her unwanted daughter as prey to the needs of the hungry man in her spouse and in the father of the unprotected child.

The relationship of the parents is highly pathological — and there is little or no communication except on a highly emotional and mostly destructive level, be it passive and inhibited or active and violent.

Here are the stories of two more women who suffered incest in their family.

Mary was a gaunt, bony, red-haired woman with an eerie expression, both of guilelessness but also of a heightened awareness of men's lust for a woman's body: she dressed in a way that would attract just about any man's eye. Although a woman of 35, she was still a child in a way: she had not learned to become responsible for her looks and acts.

"My father, who abused me for years, giving me coffee for the evening meal so I would not go to sleep when mama went cleaning at the factory, still looks at me with an openly admiring look when I come to visit my aged parents. He strips me with his eyes, he pats me, he rests his hand on my shoulders, and when I feel that he still knows no limits I look him squarely in the eyes and say 'Papa, just remember, I'm your daughter.' "

Mary's mother, she says, has been interested in esoterics for ages (she has vacated this earthly plane, so to speak) and has become excellent at massage (she uses her love for touch in an indirect way and only on others, remaining quite passive with her husband and in her relationship to her many daughters).

Katja is the oldest and most competent daughter of an industrial tycoon and was working in his firm up to three years ago, when her younger sister, who had been sexually abused by their father, told her everything that had happened. Katja then began to see the inside of things in her family. Then her father quietly told her that the firm would not be turned over to all four children (three of whom were daughters) but only to the son – less gifted businesswise, but much more submissive and thus willing to let his seventy-year-old boss and father order him about. When Katja realized that her mother was too weak to defend her interests, both as a woman and as a business partner, she cut loose from the family business and set up on her own. During therapy Katja revealed with great shame that her father had made overtures to her too when she was eighteen – they had been together in a hotel during a business trip. This helped her sever ties with a family that seemed so pathological she didn't know how to handle them.

* * *

Sexual abuse, whether of children or of women, has existed for a very long time. In many societies it has become a habit. It is an expression of ignorance and of a profound lack of respect for human beings, both other people and oneself.

Children, particularly, have not been perceived as complete human beings up to this century. The Declaration of Children's Rights is a recent and fragile creation! Thus, there has been no real awareness of the oneness of humanity – children, women, minorities and old people have been excluded and are often unaware themselves of their rights and needs as human beings.

A new phenomenon is the appalling lack of restraint of many men (and sometimes of women too) when confronted with their sexual appetites. Neither religious, nor social, nor traditional, nor judicial restraints can hinder some people from attempting to satisfy their sexual impulses on whatever weak and powerless human being happens to cross their path.

What is to be done? What can we do?

First, we can stop denying the fact and begin to assess it as being part of the human condition today. Only when we stop denying it can we begin to work effectively on the situation. Only then will be able to put aside the crippling emotions of shame, humiliation, powerlessness and extreme hurt.

Second, we can begin to educate ourselves to respect human beings, particularly the weak and dependent. We will have to begin to work consciously on all our relationships, particularly in our own families. This spiritual effort will begin to affect our surroundings. Fear, hate and other mutilating feelings for ourselves and others will be slowly transformed.

Third, as a result of our efforts, the soul will come to understand the need for religion (providing it is a living religion) and its profound transforming influence on human beings and on social bonds. The destructive habit of sexual abuse, i.e. the use of power and domination instead of love and trust, will slowly be transformed into bonds characterized by human dignity.

Fourth, children and adolescents should learn the profound significance of sexuality, and how to discern between meaningful sexuality within a human relationship of equals, and expressions of power or control.

Fifth, people must learn to become active in refusing all situations that lend themselves to sexual abuse. They must learn to defend themselves – to shout, to bite, to attract help, to walk out of abusive situations and relationships and seek help actively.

Sixth, children, and most of all, women, need to be reminded of their innate human dignity, and the right that goes with it not to be used as an object. When people learn to rely on their dignity, they will also be able to build up self-esteem and self-worth.

Seventh, when confronted with abuse, all human beings must learn to label it as such and to recognize it as degrading. They must learn to break the taboo and speak out about the abuse. Although the perpetrators are usually victims themselves – both of other people and of their own life circumstances – they are still responsible for what they do and as such must be brought to account for their actions. Speaking out does not mean making a sensation in the media or talking randomly to just anybody. One should learn to speak effectively, to the right people and in the proper terms. This may mean choosing someone outside the family, if the abuse is being carried out by a member of the family, as other members may be unable to face the issue.

Eighth, the victims or so-called survivors of these acts must learn to turn to competent persons who can help them develop enough self-esteem and courage to defend their rights and formulate the accusation. For small children this may often be impossible. But public help-lines are being set up more frequently and more and more institutions are willing to learn how to help these mutilated people – often mutilated for life.

Since the subject of incest is coming more out into the open, it has to be dealt with, frankly, openly, and in a non-judgemental way. In the end, the whole family – the perpetrator, the spouse and the child – are victims, victims of an old way of wielding power in the family: the decadent patriarchal system.

Perversion and the fear of it

Perversion, sodomy, fetishism . . . Our imagination and knowledge is lost in a cloud of wonder, awe – and ignorance!

Perversity can be said to be a stage of immaturity in human beings: instead of maturing into competent and responsible other-centred adults, they remain fixed at a stage of ego-centricity, self-centredness and suffering.

Many theories have been created, and restructured, to help people come to grips with this subject which seems to hold never-ending fascination for some. Still, knowledge and theory do not, of themselves, help us to understand human beings who are suffering, nor do they help us to feel compassion or reach out to the person stranded with a perversion. I would like to suggest a different approach.

I remember my feeling of helplessness when, some years ago, the parents of a girl of seventeen came to me complaining about the lesbian habits of their young daughter. What would I be able to do with a girl who at such an early age was determined to be a lesbian? The girl came politely, we talked, but it was evident that she was not going to open up. She was confidently "selling" her lesbian habits to me instead of speaking of pain and suffering.

Then I took my last chance – I phoned her mother and asked her to come and see me. The mother had grown up with three other sisters in a single-parent family. Her father had died early. With this first daughter of hers she relived many of her own fears of loss and pain during childhood and adolescence. We began to speak about her piercing fear that her daughter, coming home late on a Saturday night, would be attacked and raped. She spoke of her desperate anxieties as she lay awake, hour after hour, listening for the slight noise when the door would at last open to let her daughter in; once that happened she fell into a deep, anxious sleep. As the mother came and unburdened her own fears and childhood memories, the daughter surprised everyone with a boyfriend!

A few years ago I was sought out for help by two refugees who lived in another country and who, to any psychotherapist, looked and acted like lesbians: they were extremely quarrelsome with each other and were having terrible rows. Evidently, one of them was beginning to change and the quarrels came about because the other didn't want to move out of the steady state.

Looking at the situation more closely, we found that both women had left their homeland and their parents at an early and tender age, and they had supported each other, it seemed, in a very difficult time of their life. They had, in a way, been stranded on an island all alone.

As we began working with the situation, they allowed each other to become individual human beings with different likings and needs, capacities and tastes. Today each one is living a separate, not always easy, life. Each lives on her own. Each one has friends. They value each other as people special to the other. Each one of them is looking for a partner.

Homosexuality often foments anxiety, but also covers up many torments. It is the anxiety that brings people to the therapist.

A homosexual once came to consult my husband, who is a therapist. Discussing the object of his visit, my husband said he would be able to help the man to redirect his energies towards other goals. When the man said he really hadn't any idea of changing, he just wanted to get rid of his anxiety, my husband suggested other therapists who would be more adapted to such a goal. The man, who was charming, said winningly, "Thank you – but I like you!" My husband then parted from this charming gentleman!

Many people today adapt quite well to their perversion because they do not sense any need to change. This is partly because of the permissiveness of our times. Thus, they would like to enjoy the pleasurable and childlike side of life without growing up.

A successful salesman sought therapy for himself, as he was infatuated with women and felt worse and worse, being enmeshed in a compulsion to conquer them for the fun of winning and not for love. He was married and had two children he loved very much, but he and his wife had been unfaithful to each other for years. Now his wife had a lover and he was having all these affairs with women. He was wooing the latest one by fax . . .

In therapy it became clear how much this man had suffered hell from the unhappiness and subsequent divorce of his parents when he was aged thirteen. His sister had gone to live with the father, and he had lived with his lonely mother who just doted on him. He felt like a prisoner of this doting mother and left her early — to live with an older woman who looked after him and told him what to do.

Towards the end of his therapy he told of his love for a woman to whom he didn't feel attracted sexually — and how he didn't want to approach her for fear that he would again want to conquer and play games. His face was streaming with tears. He spoke of his weaknesses, but that it felt good to speak of them. This man, deep down, was in great pain and had not learned to express pain, disappointment, failure, weaknesses.

His latent homosexuality was never mentioned as such, but we spoke of his desire to be near to his father, of his disappointment in never reaching that ideal, and of his struggle to confront his father (he had a huge row along the way). From a man with perverse relationships with women and who suffered from latent homosexuality, he became a person suffering consciously.

The great majority of people are ignorant of perversity; many feel that deep down they would not be up to facing the theme with all its doubts, uncertainties, anxiety and fears. Will they not find that they themselves are harbouring some dark feat of homosexuality, sadism or other perversity in the recesses of their heart? To hide these fears many people shy away from the subject or even plunge into vituperation of homosexuals. Such behaviour shows the profound anxieties of people in facing things in their own life that may not be so clear-cut. It is painful to face oneself!

It is a sign of strength and moral cleanliness on the one hand not to condone perversity, most of all the homosexual expression of the instinct to love, and on the other to reach out with compassion and understanding towards people thus afflicted and to help them out of their predicament, most of all when there is much deep-seated suffering and anxiety.

Laurence had just become a Bahá'í. He was imbued with the ideals of the Bahá'í Faith and had great love for Bahá'u'lláh, the Author of this Faith. This love prompted him to seek therapy for his homosexual attitude and to rid himself of years of homosexual relationships. He was determined and, sustained by his great love for Bahá'u'lláh, convinced that he would be able to change and redirect his energies in new ways. He faced many things in himself that he had been unaware of, most of all in his childhood relationships.

Laurence remained radiant, active, and confident that some day he would meet a life companion, a woman to his liking, and would be able to respond to her. This man was courageous: he had faith, he faced his problems, he was not to be discouraged from attaining his goals, and he remained radiant in trials!

Perversity is not something that only happens to other people; it is not part of the dark side of sick people and the unknown, as we may tend to see it. In this dark epoch of transition perversity is at our door, in our families and in ourselves.

Perversity is a possibility in most people's lives. The risk of it exists in our unconscious. The challenge faces us unexpectedly. Are we ready to face these facts? Perversion may exist in us or our family members or our friends as an unguarded willingness to plunge into adventure, into the unknown, to investigate the forbidden. It may be lying in wait for us in a moment of despair or loneliness or boredom.

There are several reasons for this danger:

- Humanity is passing through phases of tremendous learning at a rapidity and intensity never seen before.

- This state of affairs gives access in our psyche to a basic fragility, inherent in human nature.

- We are not conscious of this fragility.

- Off guard, and rather smug, we have not availed ourselves of the necessary protection, both psychological and spiritual.

- Adolescents and young people go through periods of terrible loneliness never experienced before. Their psychic forces are over-stretched, at risk of bursting. This state of affairs creates an openness for affection at any price, particularly as, in most families, at the time of adolescence tension is rife and true affection is at a low ebb.

- Adolescents can thus be tempted into perversity by adults who abuse them, often under cover of being a parent, a relative, a guardian, a teacher or a clergyman.

- During such periods of loneliness, and during rather innocent encounters, adolescents can form habits which then, if the loneliness and despair continue, become set.

- Worse, parents who are obsessed by a fear of perversity, who all of a sudden mistrust their offspring and suspect hidden dangers everywhere, will push adolescents towards the unknown, towards adventure. In search of affection and warmth, they will be open to perverse actions for no other reason but the feeling of rejection by their parents. They feel misunderstood. They do not understand their parents' fear, but feel only the rejection and mistrust.

- For parents to harbour this fear, often subconsciously, there must be in them a matrix or a gap that has never been filled with confidence and the ability to guard against perversity. Fear is a powerful channel that creates the action in the next generation. Most parents are unaware of the fact of their fear, which becomes self-fulfilling and creates the very behaviour in the child that the parents find most horrendous. Fear precipitates things. However, confidence and the capacity to weather hard times with equanimity and trust will see adolescents and parents through extremely rough times.

- Many civilizations foster homosexuality. Societies where men only meet with men and women only share time and space with women, and where mixed sex encounters are limited to the intimacy of the family, often encourage the development of homosexual behaviour.

- Isolation and the absence of knowledge, culture and refinement, in an intellectual and spiritual sense, prevent people from associating with others and learning social skills which in turn will help them to find friends of both sexes and then to select a mate.

- Many men in exclusively male settings, such as football or baseball teams, or in the navy, army, or police where women are conspicuous by their absence, unconsciously slide into a need for all-male, "virile" relationships. These relationships are encouraged, or are part of the setting. The same holds for states of isolation for both sexes, as in prison, or out in the wilds, etc. These settings lead to a dearth of true relationship and feeling in the person, who then finds it difficult to cultivate more refined relationships.

- Many women, in their cosiness and chattiness with neighbours and family members, cultivate latent "homosexual" aspects, especially if they are in despair in their marital relationship.

Today, what is termed latent homosexuality affects many a right-thinking person. It is part of our modern predicament. We have left the shelter of patriarchy and a society with religious traditions – comforting because they were rigidly structured and familiar, albeit decadent and perverse in themselves, while the skills of friendship with both sexes and refined relationships with the other sex have not yet been learned! The spiritual setting necessary for the development of such skills has just begun to bud, I believe, in this new era. But we need courage to face the unknown. Courage stems from faith.

Perversity certainly should not be condoned. But must we judge the homosexual, the transsexual . . .? It is natural and good not to encourage behaviour that, in adults, is against nature. It is natural not to pass judgement on a person thus afflicted. The Bahá'í teachings on this subject can be summarized thus:

. . . homosexuals are not the only segment of human society labouring at this task [to prepare his soul for the other worlds of God] — every human being is beset by such inner promptings as pride, greed, selfishness, lustful heterosexual or homosexual desires . . .[3]

6

Pain and development

My parents and I

It may seem irrelevant to bring our parents into it when we think about our own sexuality and our relationship with our partner. What on earth does my sexuality have to do with my parents? Could it have anything to do with their relationship with each other, with their individual conduct, with the way they behave with each other and with members of the opposite sex?

A crisis in a relationship, including a crisis in sexuality within the relationship, is often linked with being too involved with the influence and image of one's parents.

"Gina was so open and enthusiastic before we got married, but now she's hysterical and overpowering. Somehow she reminds me of my mother!"

"Peter used to be tender and cooperative, but now we've got married he's become monosyllabic and rather authoritarian — just like my father!"

Newly-weds — and already deep in doubt and pain! No wonder these feelings also have a deep impact on budding sexual activity.

The conduct of our spouse may remind us not only of our parent of the opposite sex, but also of the significant parent, for instance where children grow up with only one parent, or where one had a symbiotic relationship with one parent, the other being absent (whether in person or psychologically) from family interaction.

Often, children are more sensitive than their parents and are profoundly influenced by their parents' pain.

Ahmad comes from an oriental background but grew up in Europe and married a girl from his adoptive country when still in his teens. It was love at first sight, and he had a very happy and creative relationship for a time. Ahmad had always shied away from his father's example: a charming autocrat to the outside world, but rather stern and strict within family bounds, prohibiting his gifted wife from appearing on stage. But, gradually, Ahmad found, to his utter dismay, that he was becoming sullen and distant (he didn't want to be stern and autocratic like his father, but inside he felt torn between his suffering mother and his overpowering father). There was tension in the relationship with his wife, and he sought the companionship of friends more and more often (there is always an excuse!) instead of staying home and finishing his studies. Sexual activity had sunk out of sight.

For Ahmad, as for so many other young adults, sexual activity had become blocked through his parents' image intercepting his own feelings, thoughts and desires. Towering in his unconscious, Ahmad's parents kept him from involving himself with his nice wife and lovely children. This image was slowly destroying his inner life.

Gianna had been married for quite some time. Her children were growing up. Her relationship with James had come to a halt and she didn't know where she stood. She was spiritual, intelligent and searching for a solution. Her sincere efforts led her to go over her own relationship with her elderly parents, and to ponder how her parents had failed in many ways in their personal relationship to one another. This was a lot of work, involving the awakening to a new reality in her model of both her parents and her husband. The process was a slow one, for it meant facing pain and coming out of a dream to face reality in her own life. Each time she went over another chapter of her childhood experiences with her parents and overcome the pain in it she felt stronger when coping with her rather tyrannical husband. Everything was painful: she often wished she'd never started and could go back into her dream world!

Having been immature, that is to say, in a state of childhood and then of adolescence, humanity as a whole is awakening to a state of adulthood and this means taking responsibility. The individual is following the same process.

Taking responsibility means to STOP

- generalizing
- feeling guilty in a neurotic way
- making reproaches
- shying away from the normal human predicament of the fear of making mistakes and learning from them
- avoiding reality, using such methods as fear, anger, panic, etc.

Following this process, we can cut loose from the negative influence of our parents stemming from childhood or often from generations back, and establish a more mature relationship with them.

On becoming a person

Many people in so-called civilized countries cannot understand what all the fuss is about when women say they want to become people, to live their own story, to exist in their own right, instead of only in relationship to a man, whether father, husband, brother or son. Yet it is not at all surprising that women should unconsciously regard themselves as things, for in practically all cultures the limitations placed on the lives of women — even where they were not actually numbered with the cattle — prevented them for centuries from developing a consciousness of their own worth, dignity and human rights. To many these claims seem exaggerated. To a psychotherapist they are not: the unconscious still operates as if these were facts. Also, not only have women retained the vivid unconscious memory of past reality, but men continue to operate as if it were still true.

Since parts of sexuality work unconsciously, it is as though you were having an encounter with history and many past generations. This can be both interesting and devastating

A person from a Muslim background, even one who has adapted culturally to a secular, academic and bland American way of life, will still be a Muslim as far as his private and most intimate beliefs are concerned. For some time, a young woman has been consulting me; she is being ardently courted by a US-naturalized physicist of Muslim background. This delightfully vivid and emancipated young lady is confused by the conflict between the protestations and the intimate behaviour of her fiance, who continually proffers his good intentions but acts like a tyrant, and bodes well to become a double-tyrant once they are married! This charming and intelligent young man has never cared to look inside himself and reflect on what he has learned from his cultural and religious background – what has been transmitted to him by his parents, who live in disunity but have outwardly adapted to each other. He therefore unconsciously acts, especially in intimacy, as though he were still living in Persia and his wife-to-be covered from head to foot in a black *chador!*

How many women have taken the time to ponder, or have been adequately counselled by wise and patient parents, over the background and cultural models of the man they are planning to marry, and the implications of cultural differences for them? How many couples have thought that after marriage they will live together according to the model of their parents or grand-parents – particularly in their intimate life? How many couples have taken the time and trouble to go over issues pertaining to equality of rights and duties before committing themselves to each other? How many difficulties could have been at least alleviated!

After commitment (which is usually marriage), many men become "macho" and many women a "thing" and they will then have to manage their predicament according to the laws of reality, of their beliefs and emotions – and that is often an arduous and painful bit of work.

In the sexual relationship, this often expresses itself, after years of gradual degradation, in refusal on the part of women to have anything to do with sex. Men are then faced with the decision of either carrying on with the family and sacrificing their natural sexual needs or of forcing women into compliance. (In this the law used to uphold them, but no longer does so.) Or both partners, motivated by a bond of loyalty or affection, and also by common sense or religious motives, will try to work on the difficulty, which in the language of psychotherapy is called an interpersonal conflict and is often backed up by an intrapersonal conflict or loyalties – as if each person was still actively conversing with parents and grandparents and not living their present lives.

The man will reason according to the following principles: "After all, I do all the work, earn the family living, have to bear all the uncertainty of being able to keep a job and support the family, and all the difficulties at work – so when I come home and have to be on my best behaviour there too, that just will not do! A man must at least be able to stretch out, read the newspaper and watch TV – and have a good time in bed with his wife after the evening meal! A man just has his instincts, and women must understand that a man is different from a woman. We have our needs and that's it! I'm not going to put up with all this dilly-dallying any more. My wife will have to choose, or else!"

The wife, for her part, may be feeling, painfully: "I never realized men were like this. I understand what went on between my parents in a different light now that it is my turn! How egotistical men are! I am just not going to put up with being a commodity any more, complying with every whim — having to wake up at 2.a.m. when his lordship comes home after a binge, and comply with all his wishes! No — I did it for so many years, even when the children were small, and I was so terribly exhausted I could hardly move — but now I just don't believe I can do it any more, it's beyond my human dignity. And I feel so much that there is no understanding of me as a person, no consideration of my wishes for more dialogue and tenderness in our relationship, not only in bed — no, I'm just not going to put up with it any more. There's a limit to everything, even humiliation. No!"

In intimacy, many couples are having to go through the painful process of getting to know one another as persons. A person, unlike a thing, can say what his or her desires are and be taken seriously, can enter into dialogue, can say yes or no, can choose, defer, negotiate or claim. None of these modes of behaviour pertain to things! A thing is subservient to the wishes of others and does not complain or claim its rights.

* * *

"Today I wanted to say no to my man, when he took it for granted that I would make love at his beckoning, but generations of women in me were shouting in my heart: you can't say no to a man, it just isn't done. Alma, my grandmother, beautiful and adamant in her determination not to let her desires and feelings speak, would never have said no to Gramp — except, maybe, to protect a child or save a person's life . . ."

Saying no is often the first stirring in a woman towards an awareness of being different in her likes and dislikes, in her needs and desires . . . To her it is the first cry of independence, whereas to her husband it is the beginning of revolt and of the end!

How does a woman who has not learned to express her feelings and needs clearly, with trust that she will be respected, express these silent needs and opinions and feelings of hers?

"I'm tired . . ." Maybe she says this because she cannot express her true feelings: When you do not listen to me and are immersed in your newspapers, your business or absorbed in TV, it makes me feel tired and lonely. I really need your sympathy and friendship.

"I'm sick . . . I can't . . ." Maybe this means: I'm sick from the feeling that you need my care but that I can never lean on you, receive your love and care when I'm despondent . . . and I'm becoming sick not only at heart, but in my body. I feel the pain of rheumatism make my hips stiff and it hurts when we make love – and I can't sleep when you turn over and snore after an orgasm while I lie awake for hours with my lack of feeling and sensation . . . a void in me.

"I'm sleepy . . ." Yes, why not be sleepy and read by myself, if we share so little and you're only interested in your football, your business partner's views and your secretary's legs . . . why can I not read and wander off into my own dreamland when I feel so lonely?

"I've got a headache . . ." Thank God this headache keeps me from thinking. I'm afraid of thinking things through, I believe I would have to act. And I'm not used to taking initiative. It makes me feel giddy and gives me a headache. I might do something desperate. I'm not used to thinking, planning strategies like my husband and going ahead step by step. I feel so very alone without his support. But why, then, do I have to go to bed with him?

Here is the story of a very nice gentle woman whose marriage was on the rocks: it had gone from bad to worse, her husband having failed in business, gone off with a girlfriend, abandoned the family and never paid a cent . . . At last she woke up to the sorry situation and asked for separation. But she was not ready to defend herself in court, as she had never, never said "no" to her husband. She had always complied with all his wishes and he had always gone on to another round of escalation. I tried to explain to her that she would have to say "no" in court and defend her own life and her daughters' rights. In the end I depicted the future to her if she didn't begin to say "no": her husband would contract AIDS, or he'd get heart or liver problems, and in the end he would ask her to care for him for the rest of his life . . . she left me pensively, and I never saw her again.

In a marriage there is a relationship between two partners, their opinions, views, feelings. But, so many women do not speak for themselves . . . so it ends in a marriage of a tyrant with a rag!

Beginning to speak for themselves is for most women the first step to feeling better and remedying a dying relationship that has become a non-communicative one. It takes courage and determination to go to the end and not to be deterred by critical remarks either from one's husband or from the environment, but to trust that this is the right thing to do and that equality of men and women is God's will!

Although women should not necessarily copy men, they could well adopt the assurance with which men speak for themselves. As a consequence of their assurance, men are not easily bullied into doing things they do not want to do. Their communication, both verbal, and non-verbal is clear and leaves no room for doubt.

For both men and women it is a painful process to break with old traditions and patterns, i.e. for women to speak up and for men to respect their wives' likes and dislikes, opinions and feelings, sexually and otherwise. However, this contributes to the evolutionary process that can make for sounder and happier marriages and relationships between partners.

Today a women may be an executive or manager at work, or even the boss – but at home she will still have to don the painful shoes of emancipation and learn to occupy her space, draw her limits and speak up for her needs. She is breaking with her mother's model, handed on for millenia, and this is perhaps the most painful of all, but it is necessary. The chain of tradition is being broken and a new model being put into action.

Emerging sexuality

It seems difficult, at present, to write adequately about the sexuality of women, for so much of it is still suppressed by fear. This fear is of displeasing men, and also of having to assume one's own sexuality in its entirety, so utterly different is it from the image of female sexuality promoted by the media which has more to do with male fantasies than with reality.

Thus, the assumption of their own sexuality very much depends on women's courage, and also their perseverance and persistence in pursuing their own goals. Yet today this is often neither possible nor totally desirable, for women do (and should) feel responsibility for the continuity of life, for the development of their children and also for the well-being of their men.

Owing to social and individual repression, women's sexuality tends to flower before and after the span of life when the family and its responsibilities take precedence – either in adolescence, or when her children are growing up. This, of course, can create havoc for a woman and her surroundings, and can cripple her life if her sexuality is not allowed to mature with a sense of balance and perspective.

In the following I shall try to depict some impressions of emerging sexuality in women, and also of the huge obstacles women will have to overcome on their way to equilibrium.

This is, in the main, a spiritual path of endeavour and painful maturing.

A woman must have the courage to live in reality, i.e. to become aware that a woman in today's society is of less value than a man. This is a hard fact, but she must be aware of it and still pursue her evolution as a person with assiduity and also let her own sexuality emerge. She must be prepared to face shocks and difficulties.

During this process a woman often comes across obstacles that pertain not only to her own life but to generations of women before her: the awareness of social inferiority, experienced both in the family of origin and with the man in her life: the fact of having been denigrated or treated like a thing from childhood; rape at an early age or incest; the crippling feeling of having had to shut many doors on herself, of having had to limit her potential and her possibilities for action from an early age; and the fact of having learned to live up to men's expectations of women and their responsibilities, most of all towards children and the home.

One woman from a South American country told me the story of her life. It gives some idea of what a woman who wants to become conscious may have to face. Abandoned by her own depressed mother and adopted by a domineering society woman, Juanita was raped at twelve years old and began having a child every two years from the age of fifteen, each time with a different man. Every time, she tended the baby with smothering care and love for some months, until she fell ill, left the child with her adoptive mother and went off on a spree before coming back to the same round. At a fairly mature age she married a solid man who was infatuated with her and adopted the three little girls. But, she recounted: "The day I married I felt that my husband became an animal and had no control over his mind and feelings. This was a terrible experience."

What did she experience? It was because she was a girl that

her mother abandoned her (all the little girls were abandoned, the little boys the mother kept). To her mind, a girl was of no significance. Her body became beautiful — and she was promptly raped. Rape was also attempted by the son of her adopted mother. She learned that only her body was interesting; her personality, mind and spirit were not. Also she learned that men have a right to women's bodies, even their sister's. She gave birth and tended her little girls well — too well, for she fell ill and could not look after them. She wanted to do better than her own mother and her adoptive mother, but not having received enough support and love, she felt unable to carry the task to completion. What her mother had done to her, she now was doing to her own daughters. In the end she married, very much for the sake of her girls, to whom she wanted to give a solid home. During her wedding night, she experienced shockingly how history repeats itself: her own husband, now that she was "his", treated her for the first time like those who had raped or abused her.

Becoming aware of what life implies for a woman and going through a process of becoming conscious can be extremely painful. Many women never embark on this process.

Many women, however, discover that their feeling of tenderness when in the arms of a man gives them pleasant if not overpowering sexual feelings and they often crave only for this cradling in a man's arms. Could it be that mothers, for millennia, have misdirected their craving for tenderness from their husbands to their sons? They have cradled their sons affectionately and passionately, but have not had the same tie with their daughters, whom they have educated for centuries to live up to the responsibilities of life. Men often wonder at this absence of a genital urge in the adult woman lying in their arms and her craving to be cradled and fondled — just like a little child.

Voluptuous fullness often comes as a surprise to a woman when she feels her baby growing inside her, its total helplessness and beautiful vulnerability making her feel responsible – and also, although she doesn't often talk about it, making her feel sensual in a way she has never experienced before. Sometimes women fall into a depression when this feeling of physical fulfilment ceases with the birth of the child. How can she possibly talk about this voluptuous, sensual feeling, to her husband?

The pain of childbirth is something everyone knows about. Do women ever dare to talk about the other side of it – not only the elation of giving birth to another human being, but the sensual feelings in her pelvis and the feeling of power when she experiences all these mysterious happenings in herself?

Then, is there any tenderness from a man to compare with the natural, fondling, cuddly tenderness that flows to a woman from her infant or her toddler nesting in the curves of her motherly body? How could a woman explain to a man that this tenderness is bliss itself, and how painful it is to feel it wane as the children grow up and will only give her a peck on the cheek, to have to renounce this encompassing bodily feeling?

Is there any more blissful sensation of give and take, of rest and activity, than the experience of nursing a child, with all those manifold shades of gentle, firm or demanding sensations a nursing mother is entitled to?

Vulnerability and anger

Humans are created soft and flexible and this makes them able to absorb new things, to learn and to change. This is a known fact about babies but remains true until the last breath of a human being's life.

Modern psychology is therefore increasingly concerned with the vulnerability of human beings and their openness to hurt and pain. If they are subjected to crippling hurt or pain or deprivation when too young and weak to sustain it, they learn to cover up weaknesses, hide their mistakes and suppress their feelings so as to survive, if only on a physical and functional level. This is happening progressively as our times move from the human and spiritual plane to the inhuman computerized situation of a society without values. Conversely, we are also finding the opposite movement: from insensitive and brutal, antisocial conduct to the more humane. Parents are eager to learn, children are becoming more sensitive and intelligent, people are looking for new values.

When a vulnerable and thus open human being feels offended or hurt, that person has two choices. He can react to the hurt and use violence, or seek revenge through passive destructive methods such as drugs or alcohol. Or he can resolve to face the hurt, suffer pain and try to face the challenge through adequate defence of his own feelings and interests without, if possible, requiting like with like.

Should the person be too weak, the hurt too much of a blow, or the relationship be a very difficult one where one despairs of ever seeing a change, a person can cut off the emotion and resort to the deadening of feeling. This will involve the cutting off of all feelings, though.

When a human being, through some influence in life – be it spiritual or emotional – comes to life again, on the road towards emotional and spiritual vitality, that person may need to bring up suppressed anger and with it other feelings such as sadness, anguish and the like.

In our society where maintaining a good public image and hiding our mistakes is a top priority, anger is often viewed as tantamount to violence. Little is it understood that anger may be justified to help a clogged relationship or a choking and emotionally dying personality from annihilation.

* * *

A marital relationship is a challenge. To expect it to be always supremely happy or interesting or successful is unrealistic. Nor would such a state of affairs even be desirable, whatever the romantic dream tells us. If human beings did actually live "happy ever after", their relationships would not grow and evolve; on the contrary, they would remain solidly anchored in tradition and sink deeper and deeper into apathy.

The most powerful impulse towards evolution in human beings is the Divine Will, through the Manifestations of God, those God-given Educators of humanity, whether Krishna, Zoroaster, Buddha, Moses, Jesus or Muhammad – and in these universal times, Bahá'u'lláh.

Thus, evolution and change, whether in the personalities, the characters or the spiritual attitudes of the partners, come through various sources. Some are conditional on outside influences beyond the control of individuals – war, famine and want, inhuman conditions in society and at work. Other sources of change are inherent in our own lives, where we are subject to movement according to the dictates of our age and our biological function, particularly if we are the parents of young children or the children of ageing and ailing parents. Loss of work, or wealth, or prestige, or loved ones, bring mourning and grief into our lives and often change our relationships.

Some changes come from our own volition and are dependent on our initiative and the desire to grow. Often suffering makes us maturer and stronger, able to sustain deprivation of affection or pain in a relationship for years or decades, hoping for a change in the situation or the attitude of a partner in some aspect of life. Far from causing permanent despair, this can bring about creativity, opening up new fields of activity, thought and feeling.

If people are not motivated by a desire to grow and by spiritual attitudes they will not be able to face the challenges of life without resorting to destructive ways of protecting themselves from pain. These include depression, frustration, substance abuse, violence, and retreating into a shell and thus losing all human qualities and feelings. What remains is a person with a mask, functioning like a computer. On the other hand, if people are animated by love for life, people and God, they will evolve and remain creative in many fields despite pain and sadness coming into their lives. They will bear the fruits of new spiritual qualities and hitherto unknown capacities even in the face of disaster.

7

Sexual development

Sexual development in children

PEOPLE used to believe sexuality was a thing that just happened around adolescence or even in adulthood. Puberty, yes of course, had something to do with it as well!

Of course, nobody told anybody of their own wild sensations and secret qualms way before adolescence, and nobody thought this could be a general state of affairs.

The sexual drive is a need stemming from an instinct on a par with hunger, thirst or the need to survive. It is part of animal nature and thus embedded in the vast unconscious — which is life on this earth!

The sexual drive, and also the vaster field of sexuality, both exist from conception. Like any other faculty, sexuality grows and evolves all through childhood and adolescence to reach into adulthood. Also, when people look after their sexuality, this faculty goes on expressing itself practically up to death.

How should we regard sexuality in a child? As a blossoming faculty needing investigation, a faculty that has to be tended to and accepted as a reality. If this is not done, it will become cancerous and unhealthy, or wither. Later on it has to be more consciously educated; and this requires cooperation on the part of parents and siblings. It needs a climate of trust and responsibility.

Sexual development

When not repressed in their natural curiosity towards all forms of life, children investigate their bodies at a very early age. Even before they can consciously control their movements they enjoy all kinds of delightful sensations and squirm with pleasure (any attentive parent knows this!). This investigation is necessary for healthy sexuality to develop. Much of it is achieved in a playful way, romping, dancing, touching, caressing, etc. All this happens in phases, very much like a perennial plant growing each year, disappearing into the ground for a time, a season or two, but integrating last year's learning and growth.

Beginning in that span of life when a healthy child pesters its parents with hundreds of questions about man, God and the universe, questions about relationships and sexuality also surface. Much of this is an attention-getting device, but not all of it.

It is up to the parent to listen attentively to such questions, and to try and fathom in what direction the inquisitive mind is probing. More often than not, questions on the part of the parent will help the child in its investigation. Unwanted information, mostly far too heavy and theoretical and stemming from the adult world, is detrimental to the immature but creative mind of the child. Thus, parent and child will find out what is the precise notion the child is aiming to acquire. Ultimately, then, it is the child who knows — not the adults.

Children are excellent observers. They can set the pieces of a puzzle together from things they've seen and heard in their surroundings. Their questions help them find the missing pieces. If parents frown, scold or judge this process in their child, it will shy away. The inquisitive mind will resort to other methods, usually more devious and less healthy . . .

Thus, parents must realize that sexuality is part of God's creation. It must be investigated, learned and mastered, first on a physical, then on a psychological and spiritual plane, all these three blending into each other at an early stage. The only task parents have is to channel this flow of energy, to complete this process or to prune little undesirable bits — but it cannot be suppressed, at any age!

The Bahá'ís do not believe in the suppression of the sex impulse but in its regulation and control. (Shoghi Effendi)[1]

Today, sexuality is recognized as one of the delicate subjects to be dealt with in the educational process. Sexuality is a new item on the education agenda and needs to be dealt with consciously and wisely. Often parents, themselves caught in the middle of the process of tearing loose from taboos, traditions, religious suppression or hypocrisy, miss the boat. They become either permissive or resigned, instead of remaining educators. Let us look briefly at some of the most common traps.

Masturbation

In a very natural setting, i.e. the home of a young Bahá'í couple with a small child, I was sitting in the kitchen keeping the young mother company and chatting away, while her little boy was sitting on his potty, having just had his supper. His mother was tending to the preparation of the evening meal and would glance over at him once in a while to be sure he was all right. What struck me was that while this little boy, a healthy child about 10 months old, was fondling his genitals every now and then and visibly getting quite an amount of natural pleasure, his mother seemed to register his activity but to take it in her stride; she didn't feel it necessary to react in any way.

It is perfectly normal for a small child to openly examine different parts of his or her body and to receive visible pleasure from this activity. It is equally normal for the parent to perceive but not to react to it. This is a normal activity at this age and the demonstration of normal parenting to perceive it as natural.

Sexual development

A few years ago some friends of ours consulted us about their six-year-old daughter. Alexia had been an only child for more than five years, but her parents had just presented her with a little brother. They were worried and embarrassed by Alexia's compulsive habit of masturbating in front of visitors. This habit had become ingrained in spite of admonition, scolding, removing the child from the room, etc. Alexia only continued with all the more zest.

We advised the well-meaning parents not to scold Alexia and not to be worried. We explained to them that Alexia had been upset by the challenge of a sibling arriving in her hitherto undisputed territory, and that she was using this activity, learned several years ago along a normal line of development, as shock tactics to persuade her parents into giving her more attention. She had suffered at having temporarily lost much of the natural attention that she thought was her due both on the part of her parents and their friends and other family members.

We suggested that should Alexia continue and want to defy them, they then should explain to her that this, at her age, was a private matter, and that she would have to go to her room as it was not regarded fit for a big girl in company. At the same time we tried to ease the minds of these dear friends, who had each been very strictly brought up without any adequate sexual education or understanding of the normal developmental expressions in a child. Within a few weeks the whole episode had subsided into oblivion for both Alexia and her parents.

These are two examples of a child's experience with its body and the reaction or absence of reaction of those in its surroundings. When parents understand that the normal development of a child demands that he or she experience the different functions of the body and also learn the social skills, they do not react or over-react to such happenings, but take them in their stride. They can then deal with them within the normal framework of the upbringing of children, knowing that one of the functions of childhood is to investigate the reality of the body, of the family and of society.

When parents have not learned to appreciate these normal learning processes and tend to over-react to them, such patterns will become consolidated and compulsive activities, much to the detriment of the individual concerned. Had they not tampered with a natural process, the behaviour would soon have subsided.

One of the very first patients I had to tend to when I was training was a young man of nineteen who indulged in compulsive masturbation. Masturbation was a surrogate for company, for relating to others; it was used to tide over discouragement and the lack of stimulation, for this young man veered between the two extremes of a acting like a recluse and being socially disruptive. His masturbation, of course, was accompanied with intense fantasies, but was riddling this young man with incapacitating guilt feelings. This man had not learned naturally, i.e. within his family and social setting, about the functions of his body without having guilt feelings, but neither had he acquired the social skills which would have helped him transfer from his family setting to the normal peer group of pre-youth and adolescents. Thus, we tried to help him in the context of psychotherapy. Masturbation, for this young man, had become addictive and guilt-ridden and kept him in the prison of self and his family of origin!

Masturbation is clearly not a proper use of the sex instinct, as this is understood in the Faith. Moreover it involves, as you have pointed out, mental fantasies, while Bahá'u'lláh . . . has exhorted us not to indulge our passions and in one of His well-known Tablets 'Abdu'l-Bahá encourages us to keep our secret thoughts pure. (The Universal House of Justice)[2]

In the normal evolution of an individual, he or she moves on from the investigation first of the body, then of social settings, to the mature mastery of the sexual urge and to using it within the marital relationship. This implies a relationship of fondness and commitment.

For a normal healthy adult, it is pleasurable to relate to a person of the opposite sex and to deepen this relationship. This can be likened to inviting a person of the opposite sex to dine out. It is unhealthy for a normal person to always "eat during dark hours at the self-service bar", i.e. masturbate in seclusion. In the expression of the sexual impulse, which expresses itself also in bodily activity, it is mature and normal to indulge in sexual intercourse with a person of the opposite sex – which denotes the highest mastery within this field – and not to keep to the stultifying experience of obsessive masturbation.

Adolescents and sexuality

All through the ages adolescents have had a "bone to pick" with their parents over sexuality. Sexuality is one of the issues between the generations. It is the sign of coming maturity and may seem alarming to parents who have not prepared themselves and their offspring for independence.

Adolescents are caught between two stools, not being mature enough to have attained a mastery of relationships, drives and sexuality, but having the definite desire for a sexual relationship.

On the unconscious level, adolescents today are having to deal with the sexuality of their parents, which very often is full of frustration, taboos and unlived drives. As they are very perceptive they can easily discern many things in their parents' behaviour, including their suppressed desires and ambitions. Since they are still so very much in tune with their parents (unconsciously at least), they are unable to distance themselves from these perceptions, and so they swing along with these unconscious overtones of their parents' relationship and sexuality.

Are Mum and Dad tender to each other or do they just coldly live side by side? Do they care for each other, or do they function together like a pair of tired cart-horses? Do they still enjoy each other's company, or is one of them happy to be out of the house, even on weekends? Do they share time and interests? Is there intimacy and closeness in their relationship – or is there a void? When they talk together, do they bark at each other with suppressed and frustrated needs, or do they respond, exchange and negotiate?

Unlike former generations, today's youth refuse to suppress their sexual drives and follow in their parents' footsteps. Thus statements by Shoghi Effendi, Guardian of the Bahá'í Faith, such as

The Bahá'í Faith recognizes the value of the sex impulse . . .

The proper use of the sex instinct is the natural right of every individual, and it is precisely for this very purpose that the institution of marriage has been established . . .

The Bahá'ís do not believe in the suppression of the sex impulse but in its regulation and control . . .

sound extremely modern compared with the injunctions of religious traditions of the past.

To the ears of many adults and elderly people such statements sound like heresy, and it is difficult for them to integrate new thinking into their taboos. Youth, though, are eager to hear this and surprisingly enough are not opposed to understanding the implications of chastity formulated in the Bahá'í teachings, and . . . "its being the only way to a happy and successful marital life".

So many young people have suffered atrociously from the disunity in their parents' marriage, particularly when the marriage is going downhill prior to separation or divorce. According to statistics, up to half of all marriages end in divorce in some societies, most of all in the West. Young people, then, are on the lookout for a sounder moral and spiritual foundation to the marital relationship. Although adhering to chastity will cost them much discipline, suffering has detached them from past mores.

Formerly, the suppression of sexual instincts in the young was enforced unilaterally, i.e. on girls and women, thus placing a heavy moral and social responsibility on the feminine sex. Throughout the world men and women tacitly adhered to and supported this distorted standard, whereas the Bahá'í Faith says emphatically that "chastity should be strictly practised by both sexes" – and today's youth will accept this, as their sense of equality has matured.

In adolescents, sexuality is often used to express pent-up anger and helplessness against parents and not necessarily as the powerful instrument it is for expressing affection, desire, passion or love for a partner. It is used to irk a helpless parent, and that's it! Havoc is created – in the adolescent, the partner and the parents. All feel badly, nobody knows what it is all about! And sexuality, being a huge force, breaks the ties between the parents and the child, but also between the partners, once that parental tie has been sundered. What is left is a void and often a desire not to be active sexually – or else to use sexuality to hurt others, directly or indirectly.

Many parents suffer a lot when their adolescent children act out their sexual drives, but are surprised to find that their children can mature and calm down overnight, it seems. This usually coincides with the parents taking their own relationship in hand and making important changes in their own behaviour.

Mature parents rapidly recognize the boon of reviewing and reliving certain aspects of their own marital relationship as their youngsters grow up. Instead of interfering, correcting and suppressing their children they deal with their own lives, thus giving their children a good example. The best kind of help for growing children and adolescents are parents ready to deal with the knots and knobs in their own relationship. This will help the children detach themselves from the parents and find their own mature relationships.

Also, permissive upbringing on the part of lax, tired and materialistically engrossed parents has brought out the fragility of young people and made them very sensitive to negative and destructive influences in the media and in society. Unarmed, their vulnerability and sensitivity naked to the world, many youth are in search of a new model for relationships and sexuality – and are desperate, for our modern world has nothing to offer except adaptation to the old model: brutality, joyless lust or dutiful sex suppressed by a guilty and apathetic conscience, all of it underlaid by the impression that sex is dirty and futile.

What many youth sense is the possibility of developing relationships just for the fun of it, exploring the mysterious, fathomless depths of the human being. Also, they have a better appraisal than their parents of friendship within the relationship and of tenderness.

If they cannot find this new model – to me it only exists fully in the Bahá'í teachings with their modern combination of realism with idealism providing equality of the sexes and a broad foundation to happiness in the marriage and the family – youth will be out to defy the adult world, and most of all their parents.

One of the best ways youth can defy their parents is through premature and reckless sex. Adults never see the challenge in this to their own valueless lives. Youth spot the vulnerability of their parents to having sex flaunted in their faces, but the parents rapidly become judgemental and angry – so then the young person withdraws into a shell of defiant distance.

Patricia was a good little girl, at least in her parents' eyes. She was obedient, nice, and well-mannered with adults, i.e. her parents' many friends. And she obeyed her parents, certainly well into puberty and outwardly into adolescence (that is, to her parents' unseeing eyes and unhearing ears!).

Patricia had the unerring feeling that her parents would be shocked if she talked like other, less well-bred children who sometimes opposed their parents' views and opinions, taking a stand now and then with a firm "no". Her parents would feel utterly abandoned by their daughter. They would not be able to understand that this was the normal pattern of leaving the nest and unfolding one's own wings to fly into the wide world. This made her quite sad. Patricia really loved her parents who had devoted their lives to her well-being, but had come to the end of the road when she slipped into adolescence.

Alone with her sadness, but still wanting to be part of the world and have friends of her own, Patricia resorted to a kind of schism common to many adolescents. During the day she was the good and obedient child of her parents: she still tried to be a good student, although she was tired to her very bones, suppressing yawn after yawn, and she smiled at her parents, was tender with naive Mum who doted on her and with Pa who was becoming old and simple. But at night she crept out of her bedroom and into her own circle of friends. These were the children of traditional Catholic families where morals and religion are written on two different pages, and where suppression and hiding were at work within relationships and the psyche.

Her friends were modern kids – when moving into adolescence they had taken a good look at their parents and had faced the hard fact that Papa and Mama said one thing (be a good kid, keep to morals and ethics) and did another (Papa and Mama had a gap in their relationship and each one of them led their own lives, had their own friends – and their own lovers). The young people had resolutely turned their backs on their families' false morals and were trying out "reality" by which they meant sex as it was shown on TV and in movies – crude, harsh, violent and lustful. They did it but were sad inside, for it didn't make them happy, any more than it did their poor parents.

Patricia, not wanting to miss out on all this and be left alone, went along with it – she had sex, for it was a kind of password to her circle of friends: you became part of the inner circle. But she neither wanted nor felt for it – it just was a password to so-called adulthood. Inside she was sad, forlorn and lost in a world she didn't know how to get along with.

At last, Patricia opened up to her best friend, a Bahá'í a little older than herself, and together they tried out other styles of friendship, cutting loose from sex as a means to having friends. It meant also speaking with Patricia's aghast parents and inducing them to evolve and understand their child, who was not bad but lost in a world she hadn't been prepared for.

Adolescents don't necessarily crave sex as distinct from friendship, in the beginning. It is just a means to friendship and acceptance as part of the group. Also, having sex on the sly, or else flaunting it in their parents' faces, seem valid to many disappointed adolescents. Parents feel their children are defying them, but deep down the children feel forlorn and torn apart. How much they would want to cry out: you love me, but you have not helped me live in this world. You told me what not to do, but everybody is doing just that. You have given me neither principles nor morals to guide me when I'm on my own. When I'm alone, I hear only the echo of your angry voice telling me off, but I don't know what to do to judge people and situations for myself.

In a family where crises are acknowledged as being part of life and particularly of adolescence, parents and children ease each other into the next stage and adopt tolerance and a sense of humour. They use knowledge and spiritual methods to fathom the depth of this important stage and surmount the difficulties together. Also, such a family will have learned to consult together well before their children reached adolescence. In a family like this, parents guide their children from early childhood to appreciate the differences between the sexes and acquire a positive, inquisitive attitude towards sex and sexuality. Together with an understanding of biological factors, they convey concepts of ethics and morals which will be able to sustain the children even in difficult times, most of all when alone with friends who want to tempt them or challenge them.

Three children lived with Mary and John. None of them had learned to hide difficulties. Many people thought John and Mary queer for showing difficulties and speaking of them. They had difficulties as a couple and their children were outspoken about their dislikes and quite frank when opposed to parental decisions. Their grandparents were shocked at these frank ways and deplored the absence of "good manners and obedience"in their grandchildren.

In time, though, John and Mary straightened out their own difficulties. Their children, having been encouraged to make their own choices, matured and benefitted from the large share of patience and sense of humour their parents had showed them. All of a sudden they expressed a need for religion and a love of learning; they had many friends. Sex was discussed in the family, and it was made clear that, for instance, pornographic films were not considered a good way of learning. The parents shared their own wisdom and experience, and their principles, with their children — and also their lack of knowledge. They spoke of life as being a challenge for all of them.

8

Choosing a partner for life

THE personal choice of a partner has never truly been practised in the world so far. Very few people have yet acquired the necessary faculties of discernment, objectivity and detachment from interfering emotions and traditional values, or a vision of what life is really about. All these faculties are indispensable for choosing a partner!

Several methods have been employed through the ages, the most widespread being choice by parents. Most Westerners tend to be condescending about this practice, which is still common in many countries. Little do they know that their own unconscious still functions according to the same guidelines as African or Indian or Chinese societies, to mention only a few of the well-known ones!

Intimately entwined with this age-old method, whose advantages, if all goes well, bring together mature wisdom with experience, is a predilection for material aspects. Parents' attitudes range from wise assessment of the basic necessities of life, to cupidity, even to the point where they may be prepared to sacrifice their child's happiness for their own greed. Thus Western industrialists, farmers or artisans, to name just a few who still strongly influence their young to marry a partner who will be good for business or social reasons, insist on the material aspects of life. The future of the family firm, or the family farm, or the social status of the family, depends on the daughter or son marrying "suitably".

The other model is romanticism. Reaching far back to the tales of kings, princes, and maidens in distress, sung by the troubadours, confirmed by nineteenth-century novels and poetry, it is now commercialized on a global scale by Hollywood and the media. This model, as everyone knows from Romeo and Juliet, is a tragic one – it does not fit reality but it pleases fantasy. Still, whole societies persist in this luscious fantasy, although its consequences are disastrous for individuals and society, resulting in unhappiness, frustration, marriage and family break-up and divorce. "Marriage to a lover is fatal . . . the compulsion to find a lover and husband in a single person has doomed more women to misery than any other illusion" writes Carolyn Heilbrun, truly reflecting the painful experience of many.

For centuries, personal choice existed only in this romantic paradigm. Yet today, the personal choice of a partner has been instituted by the founder of the Bahá'í Faith, Bahá'u'lláh. In the words of 'Abdu'l-Bahá:

. . . first thou must choose one who is pleasing to thee, and then the matter is subject to the consent of father and mother. Before thou makest thy choice, they have no right to interfere.[1]

This is the first time in religious history that personal choice comes first, consent of parents second:

Desiring to establish love, unity and harmony amidst Our servants, We have conditioned it, once the couple's wish is known, upon the permission of their parents, lest enmity and rancour should arise amongst them.[2]

Thus says Bahá'u'lláh in his Book of Laws. The Universal House of Justice, supreme institution of the worldwide Bahá'í community, has explained that this law of parental consent is "a law of great importance affecting the very foundations of human society".[3]

For the first time in history the modes of choice of partner, i.e. the personal and the parental one, have been institutionalized and set in relation to one another. So unique is this new mode that it takes generations and centuries to come to grips with it and to understand its profound contribution to a new model of marriage, an enlarged family and healthier society.

The Bahá'í vision of choice of partner is both spiritual and realistic, but not materialistic or superficial.

Superficial attractions are those most often commercialized today — such as outward beauty, an air of manliness or the aura of femininity in a bodily sense, "sexiness", or else wealth, prestige, titles and social standing. It is certainly normal to be attracted by beauty, but not to fall for beauty to the exclusion of all other considerations. Material means can permit greater service in other fields, but choice based on riches without regarding character is certainly a grave error and has provided many fine plots for novels.

Earlier in this book I wrote about some characters who are incompatible with each other. Studying each other's character and getting to know each other is very important, as marriage implies living together and sharing space, time, possessions, relationships, and interests. All this brings the inmost character to the fore and the marriage relationship will test character to the utmost!

Each must . . . exercise the utmost care to become thoroughly acquainted with the character of the other . . .[4]

Here, in the words of 'Abdu'l-Bahá, is the quintessence of an all-encompassing maxim to be heeded most carefully before settling the question of the choice of a partner.

"A couple should study each other's character and spend time getting to know each other before they decide to marry," according to the Universal House of Justice.[5] Another injunction was formulated by 'Abdu'l-Bahá when addressing a man who wanted to find a partner: "Before choosing a wife a man must think soberly . . ."

This is quite contrary to all notions of romantic love, where people fall headlong in love and resolutely set aside any sober reflection at all! The romantic view is in favour of following one's emotions blindly and taking these as the sole guide in the art of choosing a life-companion.

Lastly, spiritual and intellectual qualities are primordial in the choice of a life-partner and take precedence over physical or material considerations. These sober verities, which a psycho-therapist finds corroborated in her everyday work, have been put down as a maxim through the masterly pen of a thinker such as Shoghi Effendi, the Guardian of the Bahá'í Faith:

The institution of marriage, as established by Bahá'u'lláh, while giving due importance to the physical aspect of marital union considers it as subordinate to the moral and spiritual purposes and functions with which it has been invested by an all-wise and loving Providence.[6]

The sexual bond is a wonderful way of keeping a marriage together and making it meaningful to both partners, but in crisis it is not strong enough to regenerate the marriage bond as a whole, whereas a spiritual and moral union can!

On romanticism

And further, man and woman should truly be friends, and should be in sympathy with one another. Their understanding should have a basis in reality and not be based upon passion and desire . . . ('Abdu'l-Bahá)[7]

The romantic relationship is about closeness and intimacy, sharing and companionship. This longing is embedded in the human being and is part of our nature. It allows us to reach out with the same deep need for communion at a higher level, to engage in the quest for spiritual realms and draw closer to God.

Romanticism has evolved since the middle ages when the wife of one man could also become the distant, idealized lady of the heart of another – a troubadour who would write love-songs to her, a knight who would wear her handkerchief on his sleeve, a crusader. Who is not moved by the "star-crossed" lovers Tristan and Isolde, Romeo and Juliet, Desdemona and Othello? – but it is their love that is eternal; their lives ended tragically.

Although so many dollars are spent in luring romantic love onto the screen for a few hours, yet humanity has not yet mastered the art in real life! But, in the meantime, many people are filling their pockets with the proceeds.

Romanticism is a need of the human heart. It transfigures mortal love, lending lustre to that eternal love between man and God, unfathomable, eternal, beyond words.

One aspect is closeness and togetherness, a feeling in the midmost heart and soul stemming from our love for our Creator, and also for our mother and father. This imprint we recreate in various forms, and one of the most touching is the closeness of young lovers. "Everybody loves a lover . . ." Another is that mellowed, honey-coloured love of an old couple such as Philemon and Baucis in the Greek myth: theirs was true and devoted love, they needed no words. Such was their love that Zeus transformed them into trees whose boughs intertwined.

The transcending of the rational plane is another aspect of romanticism. It heightens the senses of touch, of smell – the linden and the lily are more fragrant in this state than they ever were – and the rippling water or the chimes at midnight are of a different quality from the day before. The awareness of another person's beauty and uniqueness makes this world seem more real than the one we usually call reality. Lovers in true love also feel nearer to God.

Romantic love lends wings to otherwise pragmatic persons. Their imagination flies, their ideals are loftier, the future seems nearer and the world more beautiful.

Romantic love creates a vision. It can be a vision of love or of the future, of a family, of great feats to be won together.

Romantic love is one of the best elixirs to coax human beings out of their shells. The timid, shy, withdrawn little girl blossoms into the radiant belle of the ball; the gawky, stiff, taciturn young man full of pimples becomes eloquent, his skin clears up and shines with rosy health — all this because they have come out of their prison of loneliness and the fear of remaining in it for life!

These are a few of the positive and essential aspects of what we generally term romanticism. What about the aspects experience has shown to be destructive?

In a couple, as 'Abdu'l-Bahá reminds us, "their understanding should have a basis in reality . . ."

If romanticism is not tempered in its aspirations by reality, i.e. a firm understanding of the reality of one another and the common denominators of that reality, love is doomed to die even as it buds, for it lacks a basis. Also, if a firm foundation of friendship is missing, romantic love becomes flimsy and sugary, without any real substance. It is then that romantic love deteriorates into rejection, hate and destruction, both of self, the other and the relationship. Thus "true" romantic lovers prefer to die rather than see their love wither — on stage, at least! But this is so not only in romantic poetry and the heroes and heroines of fiction: it often also applies to young people, so fragile and so greatly desiring to love and be loved, yet sensing so much difficulty in working through to a rooting of their love in reality.

This may be one of the reasons that Bahá'ís believe it essential to investigate reality when it comes to the choice of a partner. Apart from investigating character, it is important to have a vision of one's own life and aspirations and to try and understand if the person one is considering "fits".

The need to develop a romantic relationship with the chosen partner is felt by many people. Often it develops suddenly and is experienced as falling in love. But after marriage, in our shallowness and immaturity, routine often takes over and the marriage settles into a material and purely physical level.

Others remain in the cocoon of romanticism, isolating themselves from reality. In Saint-Exupéry's words, this is a couple who is looking into each other's eyes, while true love is to look together in the same direction. Thus, true love is togetherness − or unity − of vision, facing reality, whereas romanticism is the creating of an illusion on a personal island, away from others and cut off from reality. People who live like this stop developing as persons and in their relationship. Sometime, along the road of evolution, they will find out to their deep regret that their relationship has imprisoned them in an unreal state of pseudo-harmony, while life is passing them by. They may experience all this as "falling out of love" and land with a hard thump in present reality.

For a Bahá'í, I believe, romantic love can and should be a part, but a part only, of a mature and satisfying relationship. It should not be misused and end in infatuation (unfortunately often an unconscious aspect). Romantic love should neither be a dream nor a prison, but be integrated into the reality of the relationship, allowing for closeness, intimacy, sharing, and the feeling of being enraptured with the affection and even passion of the partner and lover.

On commitment

Various phenomena today are both alarming and thought-provoking:

- many people cannot commit themselves to a mature relationship. They remain single, unhappy and lonely.

- many couples are unable to weather a serious crisis. They fall apart, psychologically or physically, or both. Often they end in divorce. A sexual dysfunction may be the first symptom of alarm and can be so serious that the couple are obliged to seek help.

- many people, both young and old, live with someone. They evidently seek closeness and intimacy but don't marry. They keep their suitcases available for immediate departure if necessary.

What is happening?

Let us go back to the patriarchal model, where socially and psychologically the choice of partner was made by the parents, mostly according to the perceived necessities of society such as class, creed, business, etc. In Western society all that is left of this paradigm is neurotic behaviour.

In this model adherence to the values of marriage as an institution had more to do with social values than with individual initiative and conviction. Social traditions, including ostracism of the outsider, religious beliefs, and particularly the subordination of women who had no legal rights either to their property or their children, made it well-nigh impossible for people to step beyond the bounds of the institution of marriage. Individual insight and conviction on a conscious level had little to do with this.

Today, with the impact of Bahá'u'lláh's revelation, things are changing rapidly. Society, religion and the parental pressure that had cemented this state of affairs have become ineffectual, crumbling or decadent. An individualistic society finds itself helpless when faced with the total lack of spiritual guidance in these matters. Bahá'u'lláh has set up another model: the one of free choice of partners, of consent of parents to the choice of partner, and the marriage ceremony being cemented by religion within a social setting. The hub of this is commitment after free choice.

This is so great a revolution that the whole of society is in the throes of trying to come to terms with this new model, but is unable as yet either to understand or master it.

Basically, there is a great urge and desire in human beings to be close, to share — a desire for warmth and intimacy. These needs lead people to live together, and there are no more ethical or social barriers to this. People do not want to commit themselves to the relationship, often because they have suffered too much from the seething but underlying conflicts of their parents and extended family. But, not committing themselves, they cannot benefit from the closeness they seek and form a good relationship!

Here are a few examples of young people unable to commit themselves to a partner:

- Beatrice, a very attractive young woman, is pathologically tied to the needs of her family and thus unable to form any healthy relationships. She was traumatized when her first partner died in an accident; she then fell in love with her boss, a married man with four children, and became his pawn. Her next love was a much older man who wasn't able to have children . . .

    Here was a girl who became involved with all kinds of men, but had the knack of always selecting men to whom she could never become committed, for material or psychological reasons.

- Robert tries very much to maintain a semblance of harmony between his unhappy parents, goes home every weekend and spends his vacation motoring them around. Tremendously lonely, he falls in love with women who use him for their own rather selfish desires . . .

- Carlo usually "rooms" with a very dominant woman when he feels battered. He's like the cat sneaking into the barn at night to lap up some milk. But, very soon, this fragile arrangement breaks up and Carlo again reverts to freedom and loneliness.

These three patterns are prevalent in our individualistic Western society where children even in adulthood remain psychologically enmeshed with their parents' unhappy relationship. Societal constraints have prevented the parents from separating, but their children are incapable of forming a durable relationship, not having received enough nurturing or mature support to become psychologically independent.

■ People who do enter a durable bond often become ill at ease. Such was the woman who came to see me because of oppressive symptoms in her chest and the feeling of suffocation one week after her marriage. She had been living with her boyfriend for seven years. Unconsciously, marriage seemed to her a kind of prison! Commitment to her was reminiscent of oppression, of being imprisoned, caught and unendingly unhappy. Naturally, no normal human being wants to enter a prison! And nobody wants to be trapped in an unhappy relationship.

These four examples of modern people, among so many, show intricate patterns of unhappy persons seeking companionship with the intention of settling into a durable relationship, but always missing the goal and backing out of the relationship again: they are not able to commit themselves, for marriage has taken on a repulsive taste. Often they are reminded of their own parents' unhappy or even dead relationship that may have ended in separation or divorce, or where both parents conducted their unending fights through the children, shifting the child from one to the other and making the child the "carrier" of destructive messages of suspicion, hate and disinformation back and forth.

Thus, many people today openly express an aversion to commitment. Others manifest evident indifference to the whole matter and remain on a simply functional level: they eat, work, sleep and have sex rather in the same way they go on outings or practise a sport. They have sunk below the level of relationship and commitment to the one of animal instincts: the satisfaction of needs. Unconsciously, they play back the many rows, both verbal and physical, the brutality or indifference, in their parent's relationship. Their conscious mind takes a leap into the unknown and is determined not to commit itself.

One finds today that this great difficulty people have in committing themselves is because they are, deep down, very much afraid of being abandoned. So they guard against this terrible hazard: they never commit even their feelings, and most certainly not their lives; they drift in and out of relationships, without ever becoming committed. Many of these modern people have gone through the terrible trauma of the divorce of their parents — and deep down they know they couldn't face that experience again in their own marriage.

Marriage has thus become a mere formality and is waved off by many as a facade, a meaningless form or piece of paper. They back out of the ceremony; it seems to be merely a constraint, only existing to satisfy others — not themselves, for they have no more faith either in society or in their traditional creed. Since neither society nor religion raises any barriers to people's living together without being committed, neither of them offers a vision fit to mobilize people's resources to master this challenge. The events of this last century have eroded social values and religious beliefs. What is left? Hedonistic, individualist and sentimental components, but a dearth of values.

Bahá'í marriage is the commitment of the two parties one to the other, and their mutual attachment of mind and heart. Each must, however, exercise the utmost care to become thoroughly acquainted with the character of the other, that the binding covenant between them may be a tie that will endure forever. Their purpose must be this: to become loving companions and comrades and at one with each other for time and eternity. ('Abdu'l-Bahá)[8]

Bahá'u'lláh has placed the commitment of the two parties at the heart of the understanding of marriage, creating a new contract between individuals and society, but initiating the process with the individuals and their conscious decision, then putting it into a social context.

Commitment, then, is a conscious act integrating feelings and convictions. This vision provides a spiritual challenge. Astonishingly enough, many young people on the look-out buy it readily, sensing its truth and worth. They pick up the challenge!

But if the challenge is spiritual the condition is practical: *to investigate each other's character thoroughly before becoming committed.*

Character is a mixture of characteristics and more or less permanent qualities. It also enshrines weaknesses and short-comings. Both strengths and weaknesses have to be investigated. This investigation must be thorough, not superficial or flimsy as in romanticism. After investigation, a conscious decision of valuing strengths and accepting to live with the weaknesses of one's partner has to take place. Things have to be weathered together in a spiritually based relationship. Romantic love idealizes or even dreams up the positive characteristics, but denies the weaknesses. This state of affairs in romantic love does not correlate with reality and the relationship slowly erodes unless substantially supported by work on reality and character and acquiring a spiritual vision.

Interestingly enough, sexology supports this model of commitment: a sexual dysfunction in a serious crisis can only be worked through if people are committed to each other. In the absence of commitment the relationship erodes when sexual dysfunction is prevalent for a long span of time.

Modern life has done away with spontaneous confidence and trust, and also with courage and faith. Thus people have quietly put aside belief in the sincerity of people and the basic potential of human beings to evolve and change.

On the other hand, psychologically, we find two new phenomena which are linked with each other:

— First, there is a general tendency for people to become more vulnerable. Vulnerability in a positive sense, according to modern psychological findings, correlates with creativity and a sensitivity for understanding people, including oneself. It will ultimately prevent people from committing cruel and brutal acts and incite them to investigate spiritual methods.

— Second, a great loneliness ensues if vulnerable people have not been able to learn spiritual methods of defending their rights and privileges.

During the infancy and childhood of mankind, it was religion that protected people from the devastating experience and disappointment of loneliness. Today, people are having to go through this experience without religion, on their way to adulthood. And being lonely and living together is a very difficult thing!

As we can see, then, increasing vulnerability leads to loneliness if not bolstered by tremendous spiritual learning, and both vulnerability and loneliness are part of the incapacity of people to commit themselves. It is the loneliness — the outcome of vulnerability — that generates the great fear of becoming committed. People are afraid of being hurt to such an extent that they will have to leave their "tormentor", i.e. their partner.

Not having learned spiritual methods of self-defence, such as a sense of humour, knowledge about people and relationships based on spirituality, the art of negotiating or forgiveness, prevents people from committing themselves blithely, confidently, and happily. Yet the positive aspects of vulnerability, i.e. creativity and sensitivity, will eventually lead them to new learning and provide them with skills undreamed of.

Another phenomenon encountered is the following:

Not only society as a whole, but each individual and couple have to go through the laborious and often long and painful process of leaving the eroded patriarchal model and committing themselves to their partner on a spiritual basis. In the process, they have to work on their character and relationship – and once involved in the process, they will never again be able to leave it or they will become sick again in their relationship and individually mutilated.

Our society has not yet begun to teach people how to form meaningful relationships, how to acquire social skills that lead to mature adult relationships, how to perfect their character, how to become conscious of their motives, and how to select a suitable marriage partner. On the contrary, it is contributing to the breaking up of marriage and family ties.

Commitment in the Bahá'í sense thus implies being able to circumvent lasting hurt; commitment means more than just a marriage certificate – a piece of paper, as young people say disdainfully today – it is more than a marriage ceremony in the presence of family and friends. Commitment is a pervading contract on all levels: administrative, social, family-wise, financial, physical, emotional and most of all spiritual. All these levels of human interaction should find a commitment and thus develop and grow.

Commitment permits the growth of a relationship, and a relationship is a new creation, through the interaction, the involvement and exchange of two distinct human beings.

Only if people have the courage and faith to interact spiritually can their relationship really grow and become rooted, and thus become durable and unshaken through the vicissitudes of life. This spiritual commitment implies, though, belief in spiritual values. It implies, too, the certitude that the spirit will work in the relationship, and also the knowledge that there will be tests and trials to be weathered.

A commitment can only be firm if both parties work on themselves and have this kind of belief. Working on themselves prevents them from meddling too much with the other person's responsibilities.

9

New aspects of sexuality

Relationship

Bahá'í marriage is a true relationship between two parties who are fond of one another. ('Abdu'l-Bahá)[1]

Who are you married to? Your father, your mother, your sister, your brother, your business, your political career?

Relationship does indeed imply an intimate, important matter! Many people have never left their family of origin. Many Orientals speak openly and easily of their passionate attachment to the members of their family of origin, about their achievements, their martyrs and heroes — but remain strangely silent about the contributions and achievements of their spouse. Many Westerners hide the fact that they are still emotionally dependent, either partially or even in a totally childlike way, on their family of origin — but it expresses itself indirectly, in a neurotic way and confuses both themselves and those around them.

Relationship implies growing out of the family of origin, opening up to the unknown, to new faces, new people; appreciating other qualities and characteristics, investigating new realities and fathoming the personality of another person. Relationship implies sharing, contributing strengths and seeking help for weaknesses. Relationship is an adventurous path.

"My husband died a few years ago of a heart attack. I am 27 and have a child. Do you think I should remarry? What happens to the relationship I had with my husband?" Sensing the distress of this young lady, a widow at an early age, and a sincere Bahá'í, I tried to explain to her, using my hands and fingers, that we relate differently to each person, using different qualities and aspects of our personality, like facets of a diamond, and that no two relationships are the same. Thus each one is unique and will endure, if it is based on true qualities and feelings. When our physical life comes to an end at death, we take with us our spiritual relationships. Thus, the sexual life linked to physical life comes to an end, but true relationships endure.

A patient of mine was very distressed about her relationship to her husband. The husband had a rigid personality and would and could not change. All of a sudden she understood that you do not, cannot change the personality of an adult, particularly if that person resists change and wants things to remain as they have been before. But you can work on the relationship. She understood in a flash that she could work on her own growth and that through doing this she herself would change. Her growth would affect the relationship and the husband would then relate differently to her.

"My first wife died when I was 56. We had a good relationship – built around practical things like having a family, building up our business, serving the Faith in practical ways. My second wife and I have had a more spiritual relationship, reading and understanding the Writings, inspiring people and going pioneering." This eminent and spiritual man had understood that both his relationships to his two wives were important to him, each in its own sphere, and that he would not trade the one for the other. Both were essential, although different.

Those who are insecure and cling frantically to their childhood identity in their family of origin will close up and stick to role-thinking (I'm the provider for my wife, she supports me; I deal with my job and the outside world, she manages the children and household, etc.) but never form a true relationship. They will not embark on the adventure of growth, of learning, of change: of forming a true, living relationship as it is envisaged in the Bahá'í Writings.

Through expressions such as: "they must make a great effort to acquaint themselves with each other's character", and "their aim should be to create love, friendship, and union between themselves",[2] the Writings imply that a lot of effort goes into sustaining a relationship. One of the important aspects of a relationship is to understand the "ingredients" of it, i.e. the qualities and characteristics of each spouse. Being acquainted with each other's character is a kind of taking stock of each other's capital. Most people waste years and decades taking stock of the missing parts, i.e. of their reciprocal mistakes, of things that are lacking, of weaknesses. The more they dwell on these the more they will witness the degradation of the relationship. Qualities are like bricks, weaknesses are the missing bricks – the holes! Basing yourself on the negative aspects discourages both partners and undermines the relationship.

Passion and sensuality in love

Love is a fundamental power of attraction in the universe, but at the human level it must be governed and directed by the rational soul lest, unrestrained, it lead us into behaviour that is contrary to the teachings.[3]

In one of His Tablets Bahá'u'lláh says, "the drunkenness of passion hath perverted most of mankind: Where are the day-springs of purity, O Desire of the worlds?"[4] In this Tablet Bahá'u'lláh expresses in poignant words the concept that passion can lead people away from their spiritual goals. "The drunkenness of passion" describes lustfulness where one is oblivious of spiritual aspects.

When I was growing up — in a Christian society, and a multicultural and multidenominational family — I became painfully aware of the prevalent antithesis of body and mind, of physical needs and those of the spirit. Later on, during my studies, the implications in human sciences, literature and the arts became apparent. During my activity as a psychiatrist I have become ever more aware of the suppressive mechanisms that have pushed bodily and sexual needs into people's unconscious but have created havoc in the psyche of many families where former generations had been rigidly and fanatically adhering to the Christian principle enunciated by St. Paul:

Do not deny yourselves to one another, except when you agree upon a temporary abstinence in order to devote yourselves to prayer; afterwards you may come together again; otherwise, for lack of self-control, you may be tempted by Satan.[5]

When I came to know the Bahá'í teachings on the body and sexuality I felt relief. The body and its needs, including sexuality, were part of God's creation and thus fundamentally good provided they were used according to God's purpose. Expressed in modern imagery, sexuality is good if "packaged in chastity", that is within the relationship of husband and wife. All other relationships, such as those within the family and among friends, should be permeated by love — that love described in the Writings of 'Abdu'l-Bahá as "the vital bond inherent, in accordance with the divine creation, in the realities of things".[6]

Passion and sensuality are aspects of love that have been particularly suppressed in the consciousness of decadent religious systems — or they are expressed explosively in perversions, thus evading control by the conscious soul.

When I was researching this book, a query to the Research

Department of the Universal House of Justice, concerning passion, brought the following elucidation which seems particularly relevant:

In the Bahá'í understanding of life, material things and one's material or animal nature are not despised. They are given to us to be used for our own benefit and to the glory of God. But they must be viewed in their own station and must be subordinated to the rule and illumination of a higher order — of the spiritual nature of man. Bahá'u'lláh acknowledges that human beings have passions; He does not tell us to erase them, but in the *Kitáb-i-Aqdas* He does warn us not to "indulge" them. The power of the passionate longing in human love is clear from Bahá'u'lláh's use of it in *The Seven Valleys* as a metaphor for the ardent love of the soul for God. Here love is depicted on two very different spiritual levels, but the reality of the soul's longing for God can be described in this way only because the love between a lover and his beloved is seen to be a valid metaphor for it.[7]

It is the integration in the Bahá'í teachings of passionate aspects of love for others with fidelity, loyalty, chastity (purity), and affection that seems particularly meaningful. Passion is not suppressed as in the prevalent Christian concept of the antithesis of body and spirit. Neither is it upheld as the epitome, the sole expression of love, as in romantic love, where it is doomed to end after a certain time because it is not tempered and balanced by other aspects of love.

It can well be imagined that in the future, as people grow and their relationships mature, passionate love will remain contained in the marital relationship and will not fade away as it does so often. Today it very often serves only the biological function of bringing people together into marriage, but dies away when people unconsciously rebel against the "prison" of matrimony.

As we understand the terms, "passion" (the root meaning of which is "suffering") can be defined as any very strong emotion or feeling. It is the very strength of the emotion that, on the one hand, can drive a person to great achievements and, on the other, can lead to excess if not controlled. It is clear that some people are, by nature, more passionate than others.[8]

Psychologically, passion is a powerful method for achieving things. Like all methods it can be put to work for positive goals or destructive ones. Thus within the framework of a marital relationship, passion in a positive sense would confirm the marriage in the sense of love and commitment, whereas in a destructive relationship, where fundamentally it is lust, possessiveness and egotism that are at work, passion would be detrimental.

Peter and Maria, not adhering to any religious principle in particular, had been living together for several years. Realizing that their tie was a deep one and that they wanted to remain together and bring up children, they married. To their astonishment and dismay they found that as soon as they were married they didn't love each other with the same passion as before.

What happened? Unconsciously marriage was tantamount to boredom, establishment, the bourgeoisie – and thus became a prison! When this was worked through with Maria and Peter, they were able to integrate passion again into their relationship. They understood that revolt had sapped their passionate love.

Usually, when people feel passion has seeped out of their relationship, they look for it elsewhere. It seems as simple as that in times of intense and exclusive consumerism! Hipped on love in its form of passion, they have a lover outside their steady relationship. When this "love" dies down they seek another, and so on. In the end they are in a state of emptiness and confusion, for passion tends to burn down – but also out! It is like fire: if it receives no fuel from other aspects of love within the relationship it dies down not only in one relationship and the following one, but ultimately in the person. We then arrive at these modern forms of perversion where a person becomes homosexual or lesbian after many years of a steady marital relationship, or a Casanova suddenly becomes a misogynist or an ascetic, avoiding human relationships and devoting himself to some obscure cause. When souls are not fed by spirituality, human beings become disillusioned about true relationship and true love.

For if the spiritual qualities of the soul, open to the breath of the divine Spirit, are never used, they become atrophied, enfeebled, whilst the soul's material qualities alone being exercised, they become terribly powerful – and the unhappy, misguided man becomes more savage, more unjust, more vile, more cruel, more malevolent then the lower animals themselves. All his aspirations and desires being strengthened by the lower side of the soul's nature, he becomes more and more brutal, until his whole being is in no way superior to that of the beasts that perish. Men such as this plan to work evil, to hurt and to destroy; they are entirely without the spirit of divine compassion, for the celestial quality of the soul has been dominated by that of the material . . . You perceive how the soul is the intermediary between the body and the spirit. ('Abdu'l-Bahá)[9]

In this context the elucidations of the Research Department of the Universal House of Justice fall into place:

"Sensuality" covers a wide range of meanings, all related to the pleasures to be obtained from the physical senses or sensations. Again, it is the extremes of this quality that are reprehensible. To renounce all sensual pleasures, or even to go beyond this and to inflict pain upon oneself falls in the region of asceticism, which the *Kitáb-i-Aqdas* prohibits. On the other hand, to be self-indulgent in regard to food, drink, and sexual enjoyment, giving oneself up to the gratification of one's appetites, becomes the licentiousness which is, likewise, forbidden in the Faith. As in the case of passion, individuals vary in the sensuality of their natures; some may need to restrain this quality, others may need to foster a greater warmth of feeling.

. . . How are a young couple, brought up to behave in the strictly moral way explained in the Bahá'í teachings, to overcome the reticence which will exist between them, even though they will be free of the old attitude that sex is despicable?

Undoubtedly each couple will approach the matter differently, in accordance with the characters of the two people involved, but it is certainly here that passion and sensuality can play an important role, if accepted as normal qualities of a human being and if properly controlled and balanced by the reason and will.[10]

Bahá'ís believe religion and spirituality permit human beings to become creative. One young friend of mine who had been educated in a Bahá'í family was about to marry a man also educated as a Bahá'í, i.e. with high ideals and aims. Before their marriage, they earnestly confided one to another that they were afraid of the wedding night, both of them being virgins and not knowing anything, practically. Being thus relieved of the fear of being unpractised, they decided to begin to investigate each other physically during the wedding night and to take time and pleasure in doing this until they felt strong and confident enough, later on, to have sexual intercourse. My friend confided to me that this process took longer than a week but that it was enveloped in an atmosphere of affection and tenderness very beautiful to both of them and part of their cherished memories.

Cultures differ both in their capacity and in the permission they give people to express, receive and enjoy the pleasures of the body. Some cultures have utterly suppressed sexual sensations and have no idea of their being good or beautiful, but have opened wide the doors to other appetites. Some cultures, for example, revel in food and drink to such a degree that health is degraded and relationships fall apart from the excess! Eating and drinking too much both create barriers between people and sunder ties.

Other cultures, often those that bask in the sunshine of warm climates, enjoy all the pleasures of erotic behaviour, treating sexual activity almost like a children's game, but ignore practical matters such as the economy of the country:

many people lack the bare necessities of food, clean water, or shelter. In such cultures erotic and sexual pleasures are often accompanied by a highly developed sensuality; these seem to provide the only form of leisure available in an attempt to make up for the lack of the basic necessities.

Looking at our world and the pleasures it offers, it seems that many things need to be regarded in a different light and with a will to learn from others. Most of all, basic conditions need to be changed. We need a new model that will allow human beings to enjoy the delights of this world in a balanced way and not in excess, which has a degrading effect on the human psyche and human relationships. Also, human beings on this planet are awakening to the state of want of basic necessities in billions of human beings. Can we enjoy ourselves if they are in crying need and dying, while we degrade ourselves through excess?

Sensuality – the capacity to receive and express through our bodily senses – is certainly a gift of God and part of our heritage, so long as it is used in innocence and with a sense of responsibility, in other words, neither abusing others, nor degrading others nor robbing them.

Not suppression, but regulation and control

The Bahá'ís do not believe in the suppression of the sex impulse but in its regulation and control.[11]

This astonishing sentence by Shoghi Effendi, quoted several times in this book, constitutes a revolution in religious thinking and religious expression. Little do even the Bahá'ís know about or even acknowledge this revolution!

What is so revolutionary about it? First, the coming to fruition of a certain degree of consciousness that was absent before (and let us remember that one of the very many goals of the Bahá'í teaching is conscious knowledge, and the expansion of consciousness). Second, the evolution of social conduct and the possibility of enforcing laws. And third, the huge increase in scientific and technical knowledge and inventions. Because of all this, we are living for the first time in human history when the domain of the most intimate human relationship and its bodily expression is open to a certain measure of freedom and can come under the conscious control of free choice, and when it is also possible to explore and understand its spiritual implications.

In all former religions the marriage relationship and its bodily expression was based on a relatively crude and primitive understanding. The clergy and its institutions, headed by men, regulated the social aspects and became the model for the social patriarchy. Women, subordinated in their family and home, were made responsible for the divine law of chastity and thus indirectly pervaded the social fabric with a measure of purity and dignity in this field of human expression.

This in no way implies that the Founders of these former religions demonstrated anything but the deepest respect and tenderness towards women. Abraham was loyal to Sarah, even though she was barren. He implored God to give him offspring from this wife, and a son was born to him. Jesus, conscious of His short lifespan and tragic end, never married, but what we know of His conversations and dealings with such women as Mary, His Mother, with Martha and Mary, and above all Mary Magdalene, is the highest expression of tender respect for their qualities and for their contribution to His Cause. Muhammad was married for many years to Khadijih, a widow twenty-seven years older than he, and was faithful to her until she died. What we know of this marriage suggests that it was a happy and spiritual one.

The Founders of religion, then, exemplified the highest forms of respect, dignity, tenderness, loyalty and love in their dealings with women in general and also in their marriage relationships. Their own example was the only teaching they could offer on the subject at this more primitive time of human evolution. Even so, many followed their example!

As we have seen, in this day and age things are different. 'Abdu'l-Bahá explains:

Divine Justice demands that the rights of both sexes should be equally respected since neither is superior to the other in the eyes of Heaven. [12]

And in another context He said:

In this Revelation of Bahá'u'lláh, the women go neck and neck with the men. In no movement will they be left behind. Their rights with men are equal in degree. They will attain in all such a degree as will be considered the very highest station of the world of humanity and will take part in all affairs. Rest ye assured. Do ye not look upon the present conditions; in the not far distant future the world of women will become all-refulgent and all-glorious, *For His Holiness Bahá'u'lláh Hath Willed It So!* [13]

In the Bahá'í Faith (the present form of religious expression) then, the intimate relationship and its bodily expression in sexuality has been freed from its former suppression, and a new, conscious form has taken over: regulation and control. Failure to limit the sex impulse has led, in primitive societies, and in human beings who would not follow the example given by the Founders of religion, to the unleashing of animal impulses leading to violence such as rape, wife-beating, prostitution and the adherence to the firm belief that the nature of man was and would ever be thus! Suppression of the sex impulse, on the other hand, has led to decadent expressions of this life-giving force such as homosexuality, sodomy, transvestitism and transsexuality in modern times, and neurotic or psychotic withdrawal of the sexual forces from expression in an individual's life! Again, people firmly believe that all perversion of the sex impulse is the right of the individual and should be regarded as such by law.

Is our society today primitive or decadent — or both? And are individuals not sunk in utter despair, holding tenaciously and obsessively to lifeless fantasies on the rightful expression of the sex impulse? But are they free to change their outlook?

This freedom has been taught by Bahá'u'lláh and His son 'Abdu'l-Bahá, and is upheld by the Bahá'ís. This freedom is a gift to the world of today, and particularly to its youth. But, like any freedom, it will have to be consciously accepted and integrated into a new life-pattern, with new models of relationships and bodily expression, and also with new attitudes in family and society, in law and custom!

Freedom not to suppress, but to sense, to feel, to understand, to preserve until the day of consummation has come within a marriage relationship: this is so novel that many young people ask me, "But what does it mean, not to suppress, but to control? My mother says I have to suppress this sex impulse or else I cannot manage to stay chaste!"

This is not an easy thing to understand. But look at what children and adolescents do with other faculties. They develop them slowly but surely, often taking months or years to learn a new use of the body until they have mastered it and can use it securely and happily. Think for instance of the faculty of balance. Little by little, a small child learns to control the weight of the body, integrating muscles and joints in the coordination of movement and stability, so that at last it masters the art of standing up, then walking, and ultimately running with confidence and in freedom! Or think of the faculty of distinguishing different shapes and forms, learning to recognize them time and again, to set them together, then to give them meaning. Think of learning to read! Even though the basics may be learned early, not until the child is an adolescent or even an adult can the art of reading through pages and pages of material, absorbing the most important concepts and thoughts without tiring, be mastered!

It is in the same way, I believe, that the human being sets out very early to master the art of sensing his or her body, of interrelating with boys and girls in different games and settings. Children's games can be both physical and social, but they always take place within a framework of chastity, i.e. abstaining from specific sexual expression – even games like "doctors and nurses" or "Mummies and Daddies" have more to do with curiosity and sexual identity than with sexual activity as such. Only in adulthood does a human being, having learned to interrelate in an open and free way, having learned to master his impulses and to enjoy the company of the other sex within an adult setting, choose a spouse and express all that he has learned, from birth, in an adult relationship involving full sexual expression. But the individual is always learning at each stage of this slow, highly complicated and intricate process – a process taking place on various levels, ultimately coordinated by spiritual tenets and principles – the individual is always learning towards this ultimate goal! He or she may be learning for 15, 20, 30 or 35 years or more!

Control, then, does not imply suppression. It implies mastery within the context of intricate learning processes coordinated by spiritual understanding. Control implies both the use of freedom and also the limitation of freedom! For a human being to be both free and limit his freedom he must be spiritual, or else he cannot evolve in both aspects. To be free and limit one's freedom implies mastery! And mastery takes a long time to evolve. In a mature sense, then, control can be rendered by the term "mastery" and thus be given its rightful place in the evolution of an individual.

Regulation implies blending the rights and limits of expression of the individual into the social context of order, and expressing a pattern of laws and ordinances. The laws expressed by the term "chastity" do seem so important, though, that they must be upheld, as the Universal House of Justice writes:

However, there are certain laws that are so fundamental to the healthy functioning of human society that they must be upheld whatever the circumstances.[14]

This simple but weighty statement made by the supreme council of the worldwide Bahá'í community seems more than ever necessary when we ponder the state of hopelessness and depravity into which some societies have sunk, and which express themselves freely and openly in the young and thus manifest a cancer hidden in these societies. Thus:

It is the challenging task of the Bahá'ís to obey the law of God in their own lives, and gradually win the rest of mankind to its acceptance.[15]

Although this task may be an arduous, often discouraging one, Bahá'ís are committed to it.

Communication as a model for body and mind

Many people believe human sexuality follows animal models.

Little do they realize that a human being is – or should be – a creature in whom values, and the workings of the mind and emotions, supersede the primitive programming of animal instincts. Had they studied the history of the evolution of our brain, and realized its immense, all-too-often unused potential and superior powers, they would agree with the acknowledgement of modern scientists and sexologists that the human being, even in sexual activity, is made up to only a lesser degree of what can be called instinct or "pulsion", and is guided to a far greater extent by such mental operations as education, values, tradition, culture, taboos, the desire to oppose, to destroy, to love and cherish.

Communication in the larger sense of the word is not only a verbal operation but uses many other more effective means. Body language is one of the universally understood methods of communication – provided signs and gestures are interpreted in the same way!

Today more and more people in so-called civilized countries have come to consider verbal communication with only relative interest: it is often mistrusted, particularly by youth!

In many non-Western cultures verbal enunciations are evaluated against the background of other instruments of communication such as gesture, mime, or silence. Moreover, people who are still gifted with the sensitivity, intuition and wisdom of experience and tradition stemming from a philosophy of life imbued with a religious feeling will evaluate verbal communication against this vaster background and achieve fuller communication than those who depend only on words.

Modern systems sciences have enunciated the maxim that human beings cannot refrain from communicating: even when silent a human being is communicating all the time! As I have discovered, a therapist sitting in front of a client can communicate through sensitive mime either that he or she is following the client with understanding and feeling, or disapproving greatly! Another therapist may convey, through an impassive expression, that he reserves his feelings and judgement to his own inner self, thus communicating to his client: "You will have to do your own work," or, "I may be bored but I'm not telling you," or, "I have different approaches and ideas on the subject, but I'm keeping them to myself". In some cultures everything is blurted out; in others communication is complex and secretive, an affair of "insiders".

In sexual activity a human being should be using many of his or her modes of communication to convey complex messages to the partner. In sexual life a human being uses his or her body in different ways, integrating automatic, semi-conscious and conscious modes of action and perception. It is not only the individual's desires and decisions that come to light, but also cultural patterns transmitted throughout ages and generations. Family lore, taboos from generations back, sense perceptions tied up for instance with the influence of "the media" or the intense exchange with peers, or parents, or authority, or cultural norms – all these diversified (and usually unconscious or vaguely semi-conscious) modes and concepts form a kind of background film to the individual's own ways in sexual expression. The individual can be either in tune or in revolt, or totally inhibited by the modes transmitted through tradition or education, example or the media.

The essence of all of this is that sexuality is the expression of an individual's choice on the background of something much wider. Unconscious messages from tradition and education have a great impact. None is as great as the totally muddled picture most people have of the ethical and moral aspect weaving through all human activities, which stems largely from religion and culture. In an epoch of disintegration of moral and ethical values and of general decadence, sexuality cannot be an easy thing for human beings.

Paradoxically, many people desire to be liberal in their sexual actions but find themselves enmeshed in taboos or interdictions they can neither understand nor accept.

A young girl, a very sincere Bahá'í, was a pioneer in a most difficult country where traditions operated in such a way that men were totally free and women, on the contrary, adhered strictly to age-old rules of decorum. This girl, having fallen in love with a young man from this country, found herself in a very difficult situation. Her friend, of course, could not and would not accept or understand the moral standards of a true Bahá'í: chastity in the sense of abstention from all sexual acts before marriage. Worse, being a normal young woman, she felt the normal urges of her youthful body towards sexual fulfilment.

She turned for advice to her mother, who had grown up in a Muslim society. But her mother, although full of good intentions, was seemingly ignorant of the teaching of the Bahá'í Faith which specifies that the Bahá'ís "do not believe in the suppression of the sex impulse but in its regulation and control" — and told her daughter peremptorily that she must suppress her urges. The girl then became distraught, torn between a friend who wanted to incite her to premarital sexual activity, and her beloved mother who gave her the age-old instruction to suppress her urges.

I tried to convey to her the gist of the explanations given by Shoghi Effendi: that the sex impulse was the natural right of every human being and that to my understanding this did not mean that she had to suppress her urges in the sense of not feeling them any more. This would be tantamount to asking her to suppress a faculty given to her with her body, a faculty that was part of creation.

Then I tried to convey to her that we have many other faculties we develop but do not use at the time; that we do not suppress these faculties but we store them until we can use them. That Bahá'ís, according to my understanding, believe in this faculty as a God-given right to be used not only for procreation but also as the expression of the bond between rightfully married men and women.

On the other hand, I tried to find out what this girl understood about the intention of her friend. She became pensive and told me he wanted to remain free, that he did not want to be tied down and marry, in spite of the great love he professed. He thought love should be expressed physically, here and now, but he would not commit himself. This young friend then seemed content with our conversation. A few weeks later she wrote to me that she was sad that her relationship with this friend had been broken off as there seemed to be no commitment.

I believe it is not easy for many youthful, sincere persons today to follow their own good judgement and ethical values, because of the complex and confusing tissue of conflicting messages transmitted by parents and peers, by religion and science, by sound common sense – and particularly by the media, which very often vaunts distorted philosophies of permissiveness or liberalism which are devoid of any meaning when an individual tries to apply them to his or her own life and needs.

A young woman had been living for some time with her perfectly nice and correct boyfriend. Her mother, a Bahá'í of good sense, asked her daughter if she had been introduced to the parents of her friend. "No," said the girl pensively. The mother then asked how her daughter thought things would evolve if her friend had not cared to introduce his girlfriend to his own parents. The daughter, upon returning to her boyfriend, quietly packed her books and personal belongings. Her boyfriend was greatly astonished! – and even more so when he heard that as he had not cared to introduce her to his parents this certainly meant he didn't want to marry her and this was the reason that she was moving out. He realized that he had never made it clear to her that he did love her enough to introduce her to his parents and to marry her. They then unhesitatingly, after having clarified the issue, proceeded to do both things!

Both these examples show the healthy, clarifying influence of the perfectly clear concept elucidated in the Bahá'í teachings about courtship, chastity, the relationship with parents and the necessity of a commitment between partners before a sexual relationship can be successful, i.e. after marriage. In both cases the clarification of these principles, combined with true concern for the person's welfare – without any sort of preaching or judgemental attitude – helped perfectly sound and healthy young people straighten out their situation: the one a basic conflict of interests, the other an absence of good and sound human communication in a couple who had basically common goals.

Sound ethical values, coherent with modern life, are the

greatest help to young people. I find young people gifted with superior understanding (compared with their elders) of the necessity of a coherent moral and ethical system underlying sexual relationships. They are completely willing to adapt their life situations to such a system, for this vision is based on reality, logic and soundness in all aspects.

10

New methods of spiritual health

Love as action

"Build your nest on the leafy branches of the tree of love."
Thus 'Abdu'l-Bahá counsels the newly wed.[1]

Most people have a static image of a marital bond. No
wonder they find it boring. So would I!

People believe they have to remain unchanged — but this is
the best way to become stale and boring and thus spoil the
relationship permanently! They have no vision of a relationship
as a living organism made up of two personalities whose
qualities, interests, feelings and experiences change over time.
Their vision is of two fixed entities living side by side and
having to adapt themselves to make things work. No wonder
people feel imprisoned and want to leave the dungeon of musty
daily routine unseasoned by change, surprise or development.

The words 'Abdu'l-Bahá uses to define love are all words of
movement: swim, soar, build, walk, move . . .:

Build your nest on the leafy branches of the tree of love. Soar ye in
the clear atmosphere of love. Swim ye in the shoreless sea of love.
Walk ye in the eternal rose garden of love. Move ye in the shining
rays of the sun of love.[2]

A living and growing relationship is possible if the partners have a goal of evolution, and work on basic spiritual qualities with firm determination. These qualities, among others, include: loyalty and fidelity (chastity), constancy and perseverance, and patience.

Loyalty will maintain the bond in spite of immense difficulties. Fidelity keeps the marriage bond pure and makes it unique. Patience will give the necessary leeway to seek new solutions, richer and deeper. Perseverance will give the stamina and constancy of steadfastness, particularly necessary when the boat is rocking and all hands are needed on deck!

Trustworthiness is essential:

Trustworthiness is the greatest portal leading unto the tranquillity and security of the people. (Bahá'u'lláh)[3]

Be ye the trustees of God amongst His creatures, and the emblems of His generosity amidst His people. (Bahá'u'lláh)[4]

Often, when marriage doesn't work, people will admit failure — because they have set out to change their partner. The more they have tried, whether boldly or deviously, to change the character and ways of their partner, the more adamantly the partner has stayed set in his old ways. Their attitude is one of an educator, i.e. a teacher or parent, and most people, at least after the lapse of some time, will resent being under the permanent pressure of an educator!

If we understand that we can only change one person, and that is ourselves, we are setting about the work to do. The best way to change oneself is to perfect one's character, not necessarily according to the expectations of one's partner, but according to those of our Creator and His injunctions in the divine teachings. As this divine standard will purify the relationship, things will become progressively better. Through the addition of pure water the relationship will clear up and become unclogged, permitting both the development and growth of the individuals in it, and creativity and health in the relationship itself.

Such a relationship is not necessarily comfortable. Those who are looking for love will have to grow and create, move, build, swim — and this means a constant pouring out of energy.

They must not keep it in their hearts

Again, in case a circumstance causes a real offence between the two, they must not keep it in their hearts, but rather explain its nature to each other and try to remove it as soon as possible. ('Abdu'l-Bahá)[5]

'Abdu'l-Bahá was the best counsellor or psychologist the world has ever had, apart from the Divine Manifestations. What does this injunction mean?

Most people are not familiar with the secret workings of their feelings and emotions. Most of all, they are not aware what happens to negative emotions and how destructive they can be if kept in one's heart without expressing the hurt or disappointment, the sadness or anger. If these feelings are repressed (kept in the heart) they create havoc in our emotions and our energy store: they feed on our energy and take the place of joy, happiness and love, and of the desire to reach out towards people and express what we feel for them.

The only way to clear the heart of negative emotions is to explain their nature to one's partner, if the hurt of disappointment has taken hold in the relationship with the life-companion.

Explanation is not only a thing of words (as typically with men) or of feelings (as typically with women), but brings the two together. This then becomes effective explanation, or communication, to use the modern term.

This explanation or clearing the heart of the "dust" should take place very rapidly, "as soon as possible", as 'Abdu'l-Bahá says. If this exchange or explanation cannot take place on the same day as the incident that has caused the hurt, it should be postponed to another day, but some communication at least should take place on the same day, such as: "When can we talk about what has happened?"

The attitude towards the partner is of great importance. If a judgemental or mocking attitude is felt, the partner may close up and not want to communicate any more. We should not doubt our partner's sincerity, even when suspicion, misgivings and doubt take the place of openness, warmth of heart and trust. Often, when we feel tired or are preoccupied with other "more important matters", we shake off the moaning or lamentations of our partner as flimsy, slightly hysterical or even insincere. This attitude severs communication in an emotional sense, and conflict seeps into the relationship, accounting for lasting tension and unhappiness. This, of course, expresses itself in the sexual sphere and can take the form of many symptoms such as lack of the need for sexual activity, lack of sensations, or the feeling of being dissociated from reality.

Irrigate continually the tree of your union

You must irrigate continually the tree of your union with the water of love and affection, so that it may remain green and verdant throughout all the seasons, producing the most luscious fruits for the healing of the nations. ('Abdu'l-Bahá)[6]

This advice from 'Abdu'l-Bahá touches on the spiritual ways to make a marriage grow.

A tree goes through different phases, and so does a marriage. Each phase has its own tests and its own charm, opening doors to new learning, understanding and growth. We cannot cling to habits from a stage that is past. A wife cannot treat her partner predominantly as the "Daddy" of her children once these have visibly outgrown the shoes of childhood and have reached adolescence and adulthood. Then, a page has to be turned, and other aspects of the relationship will come to the fore and acquire strength, giving new lustre to the relationship – and a new measure of zest to life as a whole!

A spiritual relationship, particularly such an intimate one as between lovers and life companions, must be tended as we tend a beloved tree. A friend of mine gave me a myrtle tree, a silent beauty, in summer with its pure blossoms, in winter when it longs for warm weather. I look at it often, tend it and care for it. Do we care for our relationship with a partner in the same way as we do for living beings such as plants, pets, children – or not?

A relationship is a living and growing entity and thus a delicate one. It must be tended daily, or else it will wither and die, be swallowed by routine, materialism, or reversion to old habits and relationships, often in our family of origin or from our youth. Also, careers can swallow up intimate relationships!

Nourishing this tree of the relationship means sharing. Sharing of experience, of feelings, of cares and worries, of joy. Ideals and visions should be shared in order for the relationship to remain rooted in the present and the future. We also share time and space. You cannot be a distant or part-time well-wisher of your life companion. Sharing also comprises suffering, and bearing with things we can't change for the time being. All this is part of growth both in the individuals and in the relationship.

Facing difficulties

Most people have not learned the art of facing difficulties. Men, usually, have learned to take things in hand and state their wishes, and if they're not met let their tone rise to a pitch of command. If things still do not fall into place, they place an ultimatum at the feet of their partner in a tone of steel-like determination.

Women have learned, through the millenia, to be submissive, passive, adapting and gentle. In this new era, though, their faculties, desires and needs, their feelings and thoughts, are maturing and surfacing. If these are not taken seriously, they become discouraged. When they have not learned to state things calmly and firmly, they are not masters of their situation, and fall into a state of revolt and despondency. Depression and anxiety can be the outcome, or the sudden welling up of anger or even an ultimatum, soon to be regretted. Women have not yet learned the art of negotiating, any more than men.

Both men and women, then, will have to learn to consult and communicate.

Another art, for men, is to become sensitive to things expressed by their partner, and try to understand them. Often they cannot understand unless the partner develops considerable emotion and thus "carries them off their feet" into a realm of unknown feelings. These seem very unsettling to men, but help them to explore new facets of life, linked to sensitivity and emotions. They will then be able to discard some of their hard shell, developed so early in order to become "a true man" and to put over the image of virility.

This is not only limited to men. A client of mine phoned me, aghast at feeling her anger welling up when at last her husband had shattered her rational defences and touched her to the quick. It was illuminating, though, to hear the husband say: "My reaction was wrong as a method, but for the first time I've felt that we've advanced on the issue of recreating the relationship and a semblance of unity."

Women, on the other hand, will very often have to learn to persist, patiently and firmly, with a vision of a broader future, and not to relent until the issue is cleared up and has been settled for the benefit of both partners. This is part of the art of perseverance – to go to the end!

There are also highly immature ways of dealing with issues

fraught with emotion. One of these is the way many people drift into fantasy or day-dreaming, and thus constantly avoid facing the issue. They will go on living with a highly detrimental state of affairs in their marriage, and will acknowledge this without emotion to their partner and friends, but then relapse into dreaming, possibly about another partner, more ideal, more loving, more caring — knowing full well that this is simply dreaming!

Another immature mode of dealing with explosive material is to suppress it, push it ten feet underground with a three-ton lid of lead and cement over it. In psychology this is called repression. It creates havoc in the unconscious and can lead to depression, anxiety, even psychosis, resulting in irrational behaviour and even marring an otherwise good character.

Most people have learned the art of viewing their neighbour's apples as riper, better and more luscious — and envying him and everyone else, complaining about their own misfortune, but never altering the status quo.

Another childish method is the one of not seeing one's own predicament, but reading one's problems into everybody else's life and history. This is called projection. Our society is full of it, for people have not learned to take responsibility for their own lives. Usually it is combined with the age-old art of backbiting, which has undermined most of the societies in the world and robbed them of essential ingredients such as trust and affection, sincerity and trustworthiness.

The following few sentences from letters of Shoghi Effendi, penned over the years and compiled under the title *Living the Life*, may set a few aims and methods before our eyes:

Each of us is responsible for one life only, and that is our own.

Each of us is immeasurably far from being "perfect as our heavenly Father is perfect" and the task of perfecting our own life and character is one that requires all our attention, our will-power and energy.

If we allow our attention and energy to be taken up in efforts to keep others right and remedy their faults, we are wasting precious time.

Ultimately all the battle of life is within the individual.[7]

Epilogue

I began this book with the intention of bringing the teachings of the Bahá'í Faith to the attention of people interested in a broader view of the subject of sexuality than the prevailing hedonistic one. It may seem odd, at the end of the book, to branch out and go further afield in an attempt to link our individual lives and aspirations with the great sweep of history, with evolution itself. But I realize that I have told many stories of difficult relationships, with not too many of the "happy ever after" variety. So perhaps it needs to be said that I do not feel discouraged in a general way, although I do get disheartened from time to time at all the sorrow and hardship in people's lives around me. However, in spite of all the turmoil, the points listed below make me confident.

This is the first time in the whole history of the planet that certain trends are becoming apparent, and will be moving into the sphere of evolution and become reality:

■ There is a vision of men and women in a life-time partnership entering into a true relationship, owing to God's merciful revelation for this day. The Writings of both Bahá'u'lláh and 'Abdu'l-Bahá have spelled out so much of this new vision — what a true relationship is, and how one can acquire it. In the human heart, with time and prayer, these Writings spring into bloom and produce beautiful things — and if not in this generation, then in the next and those to come! It is an ongoing process that has now been started and will not end.

Thus people will prize the relationship they are building with their partner; they will not become despondent, but continue building as if it were a home or a garden, ever to be made beautiful. Not only will this relationship become their haven — a haven they can take with them wherever they go, independent of material things — but it is real, and can be sensed by people who associate with such a couple. Young people today are ever more alert and sensitive to this kind of "haven" than to all the "consumer durables" in the world.

■ Children will sense the honesty and trustworthiness of the relationship of their parents: hypocrisy and deceitfulness will not turn them away at an early age. In spite of suffering and sometimes sadness, they will not feel despairing any more, as they will know that their parents want to work on their relationship and are not giving up. It is when parents give up that children enter despair.

Each child can then establish a separate relationship with each parent according to the child's own qualities and characteristics, and can cherish this relationship for its own value, instead of having to be the guarantor of the shallow or weak relationship of despairing parents, holding the parents together against all odds.

Children will then not feel it necessary to resort to the kinds of negative stratagems so common today, such as dropping out of school, doing drugs, or crime. They will be able to go about their own business in the confidence that their parents know what they are doing, that they will not give up, and that they will go on working on their relationship despite the feeling that they are crawling through an endless dark tunnel under the Alps!

■ People will learn to welcome a crisis instead of fearing it. A crisis is always painful, but at the same time it is beneficial, in that old and useless material in ourselves is being discarded so that we can become soft and creative, turned towards the future.

■ A new realization of the dignity of men and women will help people to maintain this precious possession. Thus, they will no longer degrade themselves by giving in or giving up the struggle to advance as persons and in the relationship. Also, society will develop a more just attitude, so that men will not be tempted to abuse women, and women will not let themselves be cowed; but each will sense and understand the true nature of men and women: to be human and dignified.

■ Women will be able to contribute in a significant way to life outside the home, and still retain their roles of being the primary educators and home-makers. Thus they will no longer have to compulsively centre their lives around men in the home and the family. They will be able to grow and become more balanced, in a new state of maturity and not of dependence.

■ Men will be relieved of the burden of being the only breadwinners and can devote more of their inner selves to acquiring qualities so badly needed in the world: loving, sensitivity, caring — for children, family members and even women!

■ Men's sexual aspirations will become more refined. They will be more open to feminine aspects of sexuality like tenderness, all-encompassing sensations, and feelings such as togetherness, closeness, and affection.

■ Women's values and visions of things will become more real. They will have the courage to hold their own and acquire the eloquence and the perseverance to go to the end of things in their quest for equality.

- People will prize chastity as a beautiful thing – for men as for women. They will come to realize that it truly is a basis for a happy and durable relationship. The hypocrisy of marriage in society today – be it a traditional, a fanatical, or a hedonistic and individualistic society – will become apparent and people will long for something true and authentic. They will not want to please others, but will recognize true values.

- Women will learn to value chastity and not to barter it for passing pleasure or the satisfaction of men.

- Men will give in to the steeling and purifying dominion of chastity and learn to look at it as a masculine quality to be vied for.

- Sexuality will be regarded as a clean matter, fit for discussion with children, the innocent and pure.

- Sexuality will no longer have a sensational character, nor be simply an urge to which people will succumb too quickly whilst giving up personal growth and the strengthening of a relationship.

- Adherence to chastity will permit people to form friendships with people of the same and the opposite sex without any fear.

- Men and women will be sensitive enough to become aware of their partner's state of mind and feelings. This will allow them to develop attitudes of understanding; a good relationship with the partner will become a most prized "possession", more important than things or appearance.

- People will learn to mature and gradually to leave their family of origin. They will no longer have to hide the fact that they are still attached in an immature and childlike manner to their parents and siblings, and thus fall into pathological states of mind and feelings such as neuroses. In a mature and adult state of mind partnership will be learned gradually, from childhood, and feelings will be allowed to grow and express themselves, even in boys!

- Sexual activity will become easier, as many obstacles to its natural flow will not build up any more.

- Partners will know that what is happening is a universal phenomenon: it is the awakening of humankind to relationships between husband and wife, and the promise that they will be able to leave the prison of role-playing. They can become creative. They will feel that in spite of being full of misgivings and weaknesses, they can go on working on this relationship of theirs and overcome barriers with time – and with God's merciful help which is there for them to take hold of and never relinquish.

Bibliography

'Abdu'l-Bahá. *Paris Talks*. Addresses given by 'Abdu'l-Bahá in Paris in 1911–12. London: Bahá'í Publishing Trust, 1961.

—— *The Promulgation of Universal Peace*. Talks delivered by 'Abdu'l-Bahá during His visit to the United States and Canada in 1912. Wilmette, Ill.: Bahá'í Publishing Trust, 1982.

—— *Selections from the Writings of 'Abdu'l-Bahá*. Haifa: Bahá'í World Centre, 1978.

A Chaste and Holy Life (comp.). Research Department of the Universal House of Justice. London: Bahá'í Publishing Trust, 1988.

The Báb. *Selections from the Writings of the Báb*. Haifa: Bahá'í World Centre, 1976.

Bahá'í Marriage and Family Life. Selections from the Writings of the Bahá'í Faith. National Spiritual Assembly of the Bahá'ís of Canada, 1983.

Bahá'í Prayers. Wilmette, Ill.: Bahá'í Publishing Trust, 1982.

Bahá'u'lláh. *Gleanings from the Writings of Bahá'u'lláh*. Translated by Shoghi Effendi. Wilmette, Ill.: Bahá'í Publishing Trust, 1976.

—— *The Hidden Words*. London: Bahá'í Publishing Trust, 1966.

—— *The Kitáb-i-Aqdas. The Most Holy Book*. Haifa: Bahá'í World Centre, 1993.

—— *Tablets of Bahá'u'lláh revealed after the Kitáb-i-Aqdas*. Haifa: Bahá'í World Centre, 1978.

Heilbrun, Carolyn G. *Writing a Woman's Life*. New York: Ballantine, 1988.

Huddleston, John. *The Search for a Just Society*. Oxford: George Ronald, 1989.

Living the Life. A Compilation. London: Bahá'í Publishing Trust, 1974.

Paine, M.H. (comp.). *The Art of Living*. Selections from the Bahá'í Writings. Wilmette, Ill.: Bahá'í Publishing Trust, 1944.

Star of the West. Vol. 11, no. 1 (21 March 1920).

The Universal House of Justice. *Messages from the Universal House of Justice 1968–1973*. Wilmette, Ill.: Bahá'í Publishing Trust, 1976.

Unrestrained as the Wind. A compilation by the Bahá'í National Youth Committee. Wilmette, Ill.: Bahá'í Publishing Trust, 1985.

Women. Compiled by the Research Department of the Universal House of Justice. London: Bahá'í Publishing Trust, 1986.

References

Foreword

1 *Selections*, p. 117.
2 Quoted in the Universal House of Justice, letter 26 March 1985.

1   The daily practice of a psychiatrist

1 'Abdu'l-Bahá, in what is called the "Marriage Tablet" (not an authenticated text), in *Star of the West*, vol. 11, no. 1 (21 March 1920), pp. 20–1.
2 Huddleston, *Search*, pp. 17, 20.
3 5 September 1938, in *Bahá'í Marriage and Family Life*, p. 14.
4 19 October 1947, in *Bahá'í News*, December 1947, p. 3.

2   Traditional attitudes looming over the present

1 1 Cor. 11:3,9.
2 1 Tim. 2:12.
3 The Universal House of Justice, *Messages*, p. 108.
4 ibid. p. 106.
5 Quoted in *Women*, p. 25.
6 *Promulgation*, p. 134.
7 ibid. p. 182.
8 *Paris Talks*, p. 162.

3   Qualities and attitudes necessary in a relationship of equality

1 Tablets, p. 455; in *The Divine Art of Living*, p. 10.
2 *Star of the West*, op. cit.

3 *Selections*, p. 118.
4 ibid. p. 19.
5 *Star of the West*, op. cit.
6 Shoghi Effendi (28 September 1941), in *Bahá'í Marriage and Family Life*, p. 14.
7 *Gleanings*, LX, para. 3.
8 *Promulgation*, p. 166.
9 6 February 1973, in *Messages*, p. 106.
10 ibid. pp. 108–9.
11 5 September 1938, in *Bahá'í Marriage and Family Life*, pp. 13–14.
12 The Universal House of Justice, 8 May 1979, to an individual believer.
13 The Universal House of Justice, 14 January 1985, in *A Chaste and Holy Life*, p. 2.
14 *Tablets*, pp. 200–1.
15 *Selections*, p. 117.
16 ibid. p. 21.
17 *Paris Talks*, p. 161.
18 *Bahá'í Prayers*, p. 174.
19 *Selections*, pp. 117–18.

4 Some difficult relationships

1 The Universal House of Justice, 6 February 1973, in *Messages*, p. 106.
2 Tablet to a Physician, in *Divine Art of Living*, p. 58.
3 *Selections*, p. 206.
4 *Hidden Words*, Persian no. 6.
5 *Paris Talks*, p. 136.
6 17 October 1944, in *Bahá'í Marriage and Family Life*, p. 20.

5 Immature and degrading relationships

1 *Selections*, p. 162.
2 *Promulgation*, p. 167, in *Women*, p. 34.
3 The Universal House of Justice, 18 July 1980.

7 Sexual development

1 5 September 1938, in *Bahá'í Marriage and Family Life*, p. 14.
2 8 March 1981, in *Unrestrained as the Wind*, p. 149.

8 Choosing a partner for life

1 *Selections*, p. 118.
2 *Kitáb-i-Aqdas*, para. 65.
3 4 December 1964, in *Bahá'í Marriage and Family Life*, p. 24.
4 *Selections*, p. 118.
5 2 November 1982, in *Bahá'í Marriage and Family Life*, p. 20.
6 8 May 1939, in *Bahá'í Marriage and Family Life*, p. 10.
7 Quoted by The Universal House of Justice, letter 26 March 1985.
8 *Selections*, p. 118.

9 New aspects of sexuality

1 Quoted by The Universal House of Justice, letter 26 March 1985.
2 'Abdu'l-Bahá, in *Bahá'í Prayers*, p. 104.
3 The Universal House of Justice, Research Department, letter to the author, 10 March 1991.
4 Fire Tablet, in *Bahá'í Prayers*, p. 216.
5 1 Cor. 7:5 (*New English Bible*).
6 *Selections*, p. 27.
7 Letter to the author, 10 March 1991.
8 ibid.
9 *Paris Talks*, pp. 97–8.
10 Letter to the author, 10 March 1991.
11 5 September 1938, in *Bahá'í Marriage and Family Life*, p. 14.
12 *Paris Talks*, p. 172.
13 ibid. p. 182.
14 6 February 1973, in *Messages*, p. 106.
15 ibid.

10 New methods of spiritual health

1 *Star of the West*, op. cit.
2 ibid.
3 Tablet of Ṭarázát, in *Tablets*, p. 37.
4 *Gleanings*, CXXXVI, para. 6.
5 *Star of the West*, op. cit.
6 ibid.
7 12 May 1925 (p. 10), and 17 December 1943 (p. 20).